Beginner's Guide to
GOATS

*Fascinating Insights into
Keeping Goats*

Beginner's Guide to GOATS

Fascinating Insights into Keeping Goats

LEE FABER

Abbeydale Press

Published by Abbeydale Press
an imprint of Bookmart Ltd
Registered number 2372865
Trading as Bookmart Ltd
Blaby Road, Wigston, Leicester
LE18 4SE, England

Produced by Omnipress Limited, UK
Cover design by Omnipress Limited, UK

THE AUTHOR

LEE FABER is a native-born American who became a
British citizen, having been in the UK since 1981.
She has lived and worked in New York, Florida and
London, and now resides in Wiltshire. During her
career she has been involved in book editing and
writing, with an emphasis on health, food and cookery.
She has specialised in Americanizing/Anglicising books
on a variety of subjects for both US and UK publishers.
She is also the author of *Healthy Oils, Aloe Vera,
Berries, Juices and Smoothies, Beginner's Guide to
Chickens* and *Raising Pigs* in this series. Lee is an
accomplished cook and has created many recipes.

PUBLISHER'S NOTE

Although the advice and information in this book are
believed to be accurate and true at the time of going
to press, neither the authors nor the publisher can
accept any legal responsibility or liability for any
errors or omissions that may be made nor for any
inaccuracies nor for any harm or injury that comes
about from following instructions or advice in this book.

CONTENTS

INTRODUCTION

Goats are mainly kept to produce milk, meat or fibres (mohair and cashmere), for showing, or as pets and companion animals. In the UK as a whole there are approximately 88,000–93,000 goats including 30,000 breeding female goats (does) being used for milk production.

If you are thinking about keeping goats, it is useful to clarify what your motives are — whether you want to keep them as pets or have more practical thoughts, for instance, maintaining them for their dairy products, either because you are intolerant to cow's milk or just because you prefer goat's milk or want to have a go at cheesemaking.

Whatever your reasons, you have to be prepared to put in the necessary work to care for them. Goats aren't really any larger than a big dog, but they are not anything like dogs and must not be treated as such — they are livestock. They aren't even the same as cows or sheep, both of which are grazing animals. Goats tend to be browsers, rather than grazers, which means that they would rather reach up than down for food. They also like variety, so are likely to at least taste whatever they encounter. Goats who live in the wild feed on leaves, branches, bark and flower bushes and love them. Anything that is hanging, like clothes on a line or leaves on a tree or bush, is 'food' to a goat. On a visit to a rare breeds farm with my little granddaughter, we bought some animal food pellets in a paper bag. We showed her how to put the pellets in the palm of her hand so she could feed the animals. All was fine until we got to the goats, one of which snatched the food, bag and all, from her hand and ate it. First there was surprise, then tears, but she got the point.

Goats are intelligent and delightful animals, but were not intended to live in the house with you. However, my mother, who grew up in Russia, insists that during the winter months their goats used to live in the kitchen! Maybe things were different then.

Goats need to be properly housed and fed. It goes without saying that they also need to be kept healthy. Once you decide *why* you want to keep goats, this book will give you the basic information you need to successfully keep them.

THE RATIONALE FOR KEEPING GOATS

Goats are capricious (the Latin name for a goat is
capra), destructive, obstinate and moody. They are
the animal equivalent of an unruly child. So why do
we like them so much? And what earthly reason
would possess us to want to raise them unless we
were dairy farmers or specialist meat producers?
Well, this may sound odd, but goats are rather
charming. They are intelligent, highly
individualistic, sociable, courageous and daring.
And they go a long way towards helping us lead a
self-sustainable life. When they are alive, they can
provide us with milk, which we can drink or make
into cheese and yogurt. Certain breeds can be
sheared to make clothing, and after they go to goat
heaven they can provide us with flavourful meat.

Your reasons for choosing to keep goats — pet,
milk, fibre or meat — should have an impact on
which breed you decide to raise.

Whatever your decision, do not fall into the trap of
thinking that just because even full sized goats are
approximately the same weight as a large dog, that
they are like dogs. They are not. Goats are
livestock and must be treated as such. But because
they are small and relatively easy to handle, they
are ideal for people who might be intimidated by
or physically unable to cope with larger livestock.
They require less feed, less land, less elaborate
housing and are much more fun than cows.

What they do require is a lot of commitment. You
must like and value goats enough to give up a lot
of time — day in and day out, including evenings,

weekends and bank holidays. You should also have enough space and suitable accommodation. Housing can be constructed or adapted, so it is mainly the space and dedication that is important. You should also bear in mind that goats live for 10 years or more and you can't just leave them with a neighbour when you want to go on a trip, so your responsibilities will be long-range ones.

LEARNING ABOUT GOATS

Ideally you should make the right contacts before you acquire your goats. Get in touch with the British Goat Society (www.allgoats.com) to see if there are any goat clubs in your area. In my experience most goat keepers are friendly and very willing to advise novices. Once you make contact with a local club, you will probably be invited to visit a few local herds where you can view different breeds and see for yourself what sort of housing is being provided by established goat keepers. The club will probably also be able to tell you about reliable breeders who have some goats for sale.

But, if you have already acquired your goats via inheritance or other means, don't worry. You will still benefit from the club's knowledge and expertise and it's always good to have people who have the same interests close to hand to offer you assurance and support.

REGISTERING YOUR GOATS

Whether you keep one animal as a pet or a commercial herd/flock, you need to be registered with Defra (Department for Environment, Food and Rural Affairs). If you already keep goats, sheep or pigs and have not registered them, you must do so immediately.

Before moving livestock to your holding, you need a County Parish Holding (CPH) number for the land where the livestock will be kept. The CPH is a nine digit number; the first two digits relate to the county, the next three relate to the parish and the last four digits are a unique number to the keeper, e.g., 12/345/6789. To apply for a CPH you need to contact the Rural Payments Agency (RPA) on 0845 6037777.

Once you have your CPH you can move the livestock to your holding under a General Licence.

The next step is to register your livestock with Defra. You need to contact your local Animal Health Divisional Office (AHDO) (www.defra.gov.uk/animalhealth).

You will be asked for your CPH as a reference and will be able to register your livestock over the phone. If your correspondence address is different from the herd/flock location, inform the AHDO and confirm they have the correct details.

When your livestock are registered, a flock/herd mark will automatically be created. Herdmarks for pigs are one or two letters followed by four digits, e.g. AB1234 or A1234. Flock/herd marks for sheep and goats are six digits, e.g. 123456. The Defra herdmark provides a quick and effective means of identifying premises from which livestock have moved. It is unique, kept on a single database and available to inspectors for rapid tracing. The AHDO will send you a registration document containing your personal details, CPH and flock/herd mark. If any of your details change, you must tell your AHDO within one month of the change.

If goats need to be moved, they require a movement licence to travel with them. Again, there is more information about this on the Defra website.

Once the goats are on your land, they may not be moved for 20 days. This is to protect against the spread of any outbreak of disease.

It is recommended that all prospective goat keepers read the booklet *Code of Recommendations for the Welfare of Livestock: Goats* published by Defra. It is available online: www.defra.gov.uk, by email: defra@iforcegroup.com, by telephone order: 0845 955 6000 or free of charge from Defra Publications, Admail 6000, London SW1A 2XX.

It is also a good idea to have a chat with a local veterinary surgeon to find out if they have any experience with farm animals and if not, if there is someone they can refer you to.

All this red tape and forms may have already put you off, but if you think about these rules as protection for you and your prospective goats, rather than pointless bureaucracy, it might not seem quite so onerous.

The biggest problem in my opinion is becoming too involved, if that's the right word. Keeping animals — pigs, goats, chickens, whatever — can be very addictive. About five years ago, the alpaca farm down the road from where I live started out by wanting to buy one pig. The farmers came home with the pig, plus three goats! They now breed kune kune and pygmy pigs, chickens, ducks, quail, goats, alpacas, Akita dogs and soay sheep, and probably other animals I haven't seen yet, all bred for pets. Some of the animals have been rescued and the livestock at least all seem to have names.

If you are still reading, you probably have enough commitment to go ahead and take the plunge.

GOAT
BREEDS

THE DAIRY GOAT

There are many breeds of dairy goat — those that have been bred primarily for milk production. Determining how much milk a particular goat will produce is impossible because it depends on a variety of factors, but it is safe to say that you will be able to raise a couple of goats that will provide a reasonable amount of milk for your family for at least part of the year.

Dairy goats are more time consuming than any other sort of goat because not only do you have the daily chores of feeding and looking after your animals, you also have to milk them.

But will your family drink goat's milk? Some people say they can't tell the difference between cow's milk and goat's milk. Others say they prefer the taste of goat's milk and still others say they have tricked people by not telling them that what they are drinking is actually goat's milk, but deception is always pretty contemptible and usually backfires.

In my opinion, goat's milk does taste different from cow's milk. It's whiter, creamier and richer than the cow's milk one buys at the supermarket, and has a different (fattier?) mouthfeel, but real milk from a cow, not a bottle, tastes different also. And goat's milk, contrary to popular opinion, does not smell. If it does, something is wrong.

Deliciously rich with a slightly sweet and sometimes salty undertone, goat's milk is the milk of choice in most of the world.

Unlike cow's milk there is no need to homogenise goat's milk. While the fat globules in cow's milk tend to separate to the surface, the globules in goat's milk are much smaller and will remain suspended in solution. When individuals have sensitivity to cow's milk, goat's milk can sometimes be used as an alternative.

Many people assume that goat's milk is only used by people who have health problems. This is untrue. Goat's milk is certainly healthy and it is prescribed for medical conditions such as peptic ulcers, children with eczema and asthma, pregnant women with indigestion and anxious people who suffer from insomnia. It is more easily digested than cow's milk and more easily assimilated. It is also particularly rich in antibodies, and when fresh, has a much lower bacterial count than cow's milk. Despite its numerous health benefits, it is food, not medicine, and more people worldwide consume goat's milk, either to drink or made into cheese or yogurt, than they do cow's milk. If you have a surplus of milk and other farm animals, goat's milk can be used to feed pigs, calves, lambs and chickens.

According to the UK's largest goat's milk producer, St Helens Farm, the market value of the 20 million litres (about 35 million pints) produced each year is about £26 million (€30 million) in Britain, the largest market in Europe. Mike Hind, sales and marketing manager at St Helens Farm, said that the market had increased by up to 15 per cent in recent years, driven by an increased prevalence of cow's milk intolerance and consumer demand for products perceived as more natural.

Dairy goat numbers in the UK have remained constant at around 33,000 over the past two years. Sixty per cent are kept in small herds for house milk production.

The main breeds are British Saanen, British Toggenburg, British Alpine and Anglo Nubian.

BRITISH SAANEN

The British Saanen is a white goat with erect ears, a short fine coat, supple skin and a distinctly feminine head which may be either straight or dished (concave). According to the British Goat Society, this breed should have 'good length and depth without legginess'. It was developed in the UK and largely influenced by imported Saanen goats. The name originates from the Saanen Valley in Switzerland, where selective breeding of dairy goats has taken place for hundreds of years.

The white coat is short and fine, but freckles and patches of colour are allowed on the skin. Generally, they have calm natures with high yields and long lactations (the period in which the goat is producing milk).

British Saanen is a popular breed for those requiring high production of liquid milk throughout the year and where large groups of goats may be housed together. For these reasons this breed forms the foundation breeding stock for some large goat farms in the UK where liquid milk production is the main objective.

BRITISH TOGGENBURG

This is a brown and white goat with Swiss markings developed in the UK from a breed originating in Switzerland within an area centred on the Obertoggenburg and Werdenburg valleys, with goats reaching the UK from 1882 onwards. There were importations of goats from Switzerland in 1922 and 1965 and semen in 1993.

The goat has good length and depth, without legginess. Its colour can range from mid-brown to shades of grey or fawn, with white Swiss markings. A medium brown colour is the ideal, but lighter and darker colours are acceptable. The head is distinctive, being wide across the level of the eyes, and having a dished face.

As with the Saanens, registered purebred Toggenburgs can be used with British Toggenburgs and progeny can still be registered as British Toggenburgs. The hair can be any length, but fringing is usually present to some degree and the coat is silky in texture.

British Toggenburgs usually have sound dairy conformation as well as being strong and robust, with good longevity. The breed is one of the most popular in the UK and is used in some commercial goat farms where cheese is a primary product.

BRITISH ALPINE

This black goat with white Swiss markings was developed in the UK in the early 1900s. It should be tall, rangy and graceful with a short, fine coat.

The overall effect is most impressive when the black coat acquires its summer gloss. The breed can be highly individual in character and tends to be a breed for goat enthusiasts who like a challenge.

ANGLO NUBIAN

The identifying feature of this breed is its head, which has a pronounced 'roman' nose and long, drooping ears. This goat has a long, deep body and an upright stance. The large number of colour variations — chestnut, fawn, black, white or cream — in its short, silky coat, adds to its attractiveness.

This is a breed which improves with age. There are instances of females breeding and milking well past the age of 12. Anglo Nubians are renowned for their fecundity with twins, triplets and even quadruplets being common when the dam is well managed.

Anglo Nubians are also well suited to meat production, both in their own right and when crossed with other breeds.

GOLDEN GUERNSEY AND BRITISH GUERNSEY

The Golden Guernsey, as the name implies, is a golden colour with medium gold being the most common, but the colour can vary from pale blonde to deep bronze. Their length of coat can vary considerably, but generally there is some fringing. The Golden Guernsey was first imported to England in 1965. Golden Guernsey goats are smaller than the British dairy breeds, fine boned and generally quiet and docile. In many respects they are ideal 'household' goats. They have a good milk yield for their size which is quite sufficient for most households. The milk is relatively high in fat and protein to make it suitable for yogurt and cheese. The British Guernsey is a Golden Guernsey-type breed obtained by specific stages of breeding at the end of which the BG will be 7/8 GG and very similar to the GG in appearance. It is bigger and larger boned than the GG. One possible reason for breeding British Guernseys is increasing milk production.

THE MEAT GOAT

Globally, it has been traditional for goats to be kept as dual purpose animals, providing both milk and meat. However, in Wales and the rest of the UK, it was more common for goats to be kept for milk production and breeding strategies focused on improving the traits of importance for dairying rather than for producing meat.

While goat is believed to make up 80 per cent of the total meat consumed in the world, it is considerably underconsumed in the UK. But as our population has become more multicultural, more and more Britons have had the opportunity to sample goat meat and are pleasantly surprised.

Historically, much of the goat eaten in Britain has been the 'waste' or cull from dairy herds. With an increase in interest in goat meat, it is becoming more common to use a Boer billy as a terminal sire (a breed that will confer specific desirable characteristics in the final product of a breeding system). Breeding Boer billys with dairy does and keeping the cross-bred female offspring for breeding will produce goats with desirable market qualities — good conformation and meat coverage, giving them more value in the meat market.

Going under the names *Cabrito* or *Chevon* you will also find goat meat referred to simply as kid or goat. With a taste between lamb and beef it appeals to many people. In addition, being low in cholesterol, high in iron and ounce for ounce having less fat than chicken and about the same calories, goat is the ideal meat for the health conscious.

The meat taken from the Boer or Boer cross-bred kids is generally better in both texture and flavour than meat taken from a dairy animal, as is true of the difference between beef and dairy cows.

If you are interested in keeping goats to provide your family with meat, choosing a Boer or cross-bred goat will give you the best tasting results. However, there is a large surplus of unwanted kids available from dairy and fibre breeds that can be utilised for the production of perfectly acceptable meat, and it might be more ecologically viable to go this route.

THE PET GOAT

People are sometimes wary of having goats as pets. They have the bad reputation of eating everything, including clothes off the washing line, roses and vegetables. This is true, but with a little forward planning all this can be avoided. Most goats can be kept as pets, although the experts never recommend having just one. It is always better to have two or more, as goats are very social creatures and one goat on its own will become very depressed and demand a great deal of your attention, much in the same way as an only child.

Pygmy goats, originally from Africa, are genetically dwarfed miniatures; they are kept mainly for enjoyment, interest and companionship. They have only a very small milk production and their meat yield is also less than that of other breeds. Their feed and housing requirements are also reduced, which makes them a good choice for pets.

The Pygmy Goat Club has set breed standards regarding size and type and organises show classes for Pygmy goats. It has its own registration and pedigree system aimed at improvement by selective breeding. An adult Pygmy weighs 18—32 kg (40—70 lb/2.9—5 st), has a maximum height at the withers (high part of the back) of approximately 56 cm (22 inches) for males, less for females, short legs and bodies that give an impression of perpetual pregnancy. They are found in many different colour variations — piebald being quite common — and actually can be any colour except completely white; even white markings on the face like the Swiss breeds are unacceptable to the Club.

Pygmies are generally quiet and docile, but there are always some exceptions, as one would expect with goats!

Housing requirements are less demanding than for the dairy breeds, since these goats are so much smaller. Kids are reared on the dams (mothers) so milking is only rarely necessary. Castrated males (wethers) make ideal pets, but intact males should not be kept unless separate accommodation can be provided for them. Goats like company, so keeping single Pygmies should be avoided.

OTHER BREEDS, TYPES AND NOVELTY GOATS

BAGOT

This ancient native breed is known to have existed since the 1380s. The name is derived from the Bagot family of Blithfield Hall, Staffordshire, who owned the earliest known herd which roamed wild in Bagots Park, three miles from the Hall.

The Bagot is medium-sized, with long hair, large curved horns and a nervous character. The striking colour pattern which breeders aim for is entirely black from nose to shoulder and entirely white behind the shoulder line, however, this pattern currently does not always breed true.

The number of Bagot goats have fluctuated over the centuries for a variety of reasons, but the breed is now secure as herds exist in many locations and numbers are increasing, even though it is not a productive breed, except possibly for meat. Purchasers of Bagot stock should ensure that it is purebred. At one time a grading up programme was operated to increase numbers and decrease inbreeding. Bagot males were used on any female goat, and progeny were backcrossed. With hindsight this programme produced unfortunate results.

BRITISH

This is the term used to describe goats that are registered with the British Goat Society, but are not eligible for a breed section. It is possible to 'grade up' to some of the breed sections when the pedigree is sufficiently 'pure'. It is sometimes the case that crosses between pure breeds are made with a specific long-term objective, or alternatively previously unregistered females can be registered as a starting point. Goats in this section can be any colour and often have a great deal of hybrid vigour. British goats are judged entirely on their conformation and milking qualities. Many of the UK's highest yielding goats and also show champions are in this section.

ENGLISH

The aim is to breed a utility goat with all the qualities that make it an ideal smallholder's animal, suited to the British climate and vegetation. The female should efficiently convert the latter into a moderate milk supply over a long period, without the need for large amounts of concentrated feeds. Coat colour is variable, primarily brown or grey, with a characteristic dark line (eel stripe) along the back. There are usually dark markings on the head, legs and flanks; white patches are permitted, but Swiss markings are ideally absent.

Hair length varies, usually being longer in males. An under-down is often grown in the winter. Hardiness, a sturdy body and a docile temperament are important. The registration of English goats is carried out by the English Goat Breeders Association, a registered charity affiliated with the British Goat Society.

ANGORA

Angora goats produce mohair, which should not be confused with Angora wool, which comes from Angora rabbits.

While other goats are double-coated, i.e., they have coarse outer hairs and an under-down; Angora goats are the only single-coated breed. The presence of any coarse hairs, known as kemp and medullated fibres, is a fault.

Mohair is a fine luxurious fibre which can readily be dyed to brilliant colours. It is sometimes referred to as the 'diamond fibre' because of its lustre and hard-wearing properties. It is often blended with other natural fibres to produce yarns and textiles. Angora goats are sheared twice a year, usually in January and late summer. As the fleece grows, it forms 'ringlets' or staples, due to a spiral twist known as style and a crimp known as character. The length, lustre, density, quality, fineness and evenness of the fleece are all-important, a product of heredity and management.

Fibre diameter increases with the goat's age; kid mohair is under 30 microns in diameter, young goat is 30—33 microns, and adult is over 33 microns. The finest fibre is the most highly priced and is used for sweaters and cloth, the coarsest for rugs. A fleece report, generated by microscope and computer, should be seen for any animal considered for purchase and the results of the British Angora Goat Society's Sire Evaluation Scheme should also be taken into account. Since a heavy fleece from a male goat may weigh 6 kg (13.2 lb) and that from a female 4 kg (8.8 lb), a sturdy body and strong legs are important. Once shorn, the mohair may be home processed or sold as is through British Mohair Marketing Ltd.

As well as Angora goat classes at shows, fleece competitions are held and craft competitions at which beautiful garments of the highest standard may be seen. Angora goats require plenty of forage in their diet (see BGS booklet *Feeding Goats*) and adequate housing after shearing and around kidding time.

GOATS FOR FIBRE

It is just worth mentioning that the luxury fibre cashmere is the down produced by the skin's secondary hair follicles, which grows in response to decreasing day-length, thus protecting the goat from the winter cold much more efficiently than do the guard-hairs produced by the primary hair follicles (these coarser hairs make up the visible coat of the animal). Thus the word 'cashmere' describes the down, not the goat, and many goats have the genetic makeup that enables them to produce down.

To be acceptable for processing, however, cashmere fibres must be as fine as possible, and by definition the diameter must not exceed 18.5 microns. Other properties are also required — a suitable length (about 4.5 cm/1.8 inches), construction, crimp and colour (white is more valuable than brown or grey). Before spinning, the inevitable guard hairs shed when the cashmere moults out in the spring must be removed. For this reason cashmere processing is currently an industrial, rather than a domestic, procedure.

The Scottish Cashmere Producers Association has been highly successful in blending imported and native feral goats to breed animals that produce fibre to the high standards of the famous garment makers. Fortunately, the required characteristics to produce good cashmere are inherited to a high degree; even so, usually no more than 300 g (11 oz) of dehaired cashmere will be obtained from one good goat.

HARNESS GOAT

Ever since the goat was domesticated it has been used as a beast of burden. Even now in some countries they are being used to carry loads.

From Victorian times until the start of WW II in England, the goat and its chaise was a popular sight around the seaside towns, especially on the south and east coasts. Used for the halfpenny ride and also as a photographers' tool, unfortunately the goat and the donkey were much abused.

The Harness Goat Society was formed in 1986 to encourage the use of a working goat, pack or driven, and to make sure no cruelty was involved.

All breeds of goat of either sex can be trained, but the Society recommends a disbudded or polled (hornless) castrated male as being the most suitable.

FAINTING GOAT

You probably won't ever encounter this novelty goat unless you watch the film clips on *You Tube* or *Google Video*. Although it is officially classified as a meat goat, this breed is listed as threatened by the American Livestock Breeds Conservancy, so the fainting goat is not used as often for its meat as other meat goat breeds; its rarity makes the live goat more valuable.

A fainting goat is a breed of American goat whose muscles freeze for roughly 10 seconds when the goat is startled. Though painless, this generally results in the animal collapsing on its side. The characteristic is caused by a hereditary genetic disorder called *myotonia congenital*. When startled, younger goats will stiffen and fall over; older goats learn to spread their legs or lean against something and often they continue to run about in an awkward, stiff-legged shuffle.

Slightly smaller than standard breeds of goat, fainting goats are generally 43—64 cm (17—25 inches) tall and can weigh anywhere from 27—75 kg (50—165 lb). They have large, prominent eyes in high sockets, and exist in as many colours as standard breeds do. Hair can be short or long, with certain individuals producing a great deal of cashmere during colder months. Common coat colours are black and white, however, most possible coat colours are found in this breed. Their life expectancy is 12—15 years.

The origin of the fainting goat is peculiar. They appear to have arrived in Marshall County,

Tennessee, in the early 1800s, courtesy of a reclusive farm worker who was most likely from Nova Scotia. Before he left the area, he sold his goats — three does and a buck — to Dr H. H. Mayberry, who bred them.

Fainting goats are smaller and somewhat easier to care for and maintain than larger meat goat breeds, which makes them desirable for smaller farms. They are also raised as pet or show animals as they can be friendly, intelligent, easy to keep and amusing.

They are unable to challenge fences as vigorously as larger meat goat breeds, due in part to smaller size and also because of the myotonia. Their size also makes them easier to care for regarding foot trimming and administering medications.

In the past they were used for protecting livestock such as sheep by involuntarily 'sacrificing themselves' to predators, allowing the sheep to escape. Although there is an International Fainting Goat Association (IFGA), this breed seems to exist only in the US.

EVERYTHING YOU NEED TO KNOW

HOW TO BUY A GOAT

For the beginner, it is a good idea to purchase your goats through a regional association or from breeders recommended by your local goat club. Answering advertisements in newspapers is not recommended, nor is buying from a market.

A reputable breeder will not only have good stock, but will be able to give you sensible follow-up advice. The purchase price may be higher, but it will save you much grief and probably some money in the long run.

You should also see the goats personally before your final decision to buy. An ailing animal can take away much of the pleasure of goat keeping, perhaps putting you off the whole idea.

The problem is that as a beginner, you may not know what you are looking at. You should have a reasonable image in your head of what a goat should look like, but it takes a good while to become an 'expert', so in a way, buying a goat is a bit like buying a car. (Kicking the tyres isn't an option, but looking under the bonnet may be.) Arm yourself with as much information as you can digest and ask some questions, but in the end you will be relying on the reputation and integrity of the breeder, whether you get on with them, whether you like the surroundings and whether you like the way their goats look.

Having said that, to become an informed buyer you should learn about the goat's body parts, what the animal's conformation (general appearance) is, what traits are considered defects and then attempt to weigh and evaluate their importance. Familiarising yourself with some key facts will make a big difference.

It makes sense to think about buying as local as is feasible since you should view your prospective goats over a period of time.

What you should be looking for in a healthy goat is:

- Good appetite and an animal that chews its cud
- Liveliness and alertness
- A smooth, shiny coat (which may be shaggy if the animal is pastured or kept in a cold pen)
- Movement without hindrance
- A well-nourished, but not fat animal
- Clear, clean eyes
- Cool, dry nose
- Faeces dropped in hard little balls
- Clean, clear urine

You should also be aware of indications of indisposition or illness. Be wary of:

- A thin goat
- An animal that arches its back
- A goat that favours a leg or limps
- Pale mucous membranes
- A rough coat, bristly hairs or shedding
- Swollen body or limbs

- Discharge from its mouth, nose or eyes
- Dried excrement on its tail or under it (which indicates diarrhoea)
- Open sores or lumps
- Long pendulous udders and funnel-shaped teats

Do not buy goats from herds that have been recently imported into the UK without taking advice not only from Defra and your veterinarian, but also from the British Goat Society.

There is a very low level of CAE (*caprine arthritis encephalitis*) in this country. All goats over one year old should have an annual blood test, so before buying, ask to see the test certificate for the whole herd, ideally for several years. If buying a kid, check the CAE status of the dam.

Also check to see whether your goat has had the proper vaccinations (against enterotoxaemia and tetanus). Other vaccinations can be used in a preventative medical programme, but most of them are worth considering only if you are susceptible to a particular problem (which your vet can advise you on). Your goat should also be wormed, preferably just before it comes to you. Don't allow it on your pasture until at least 24 hours after it has been wormed.

There are all sorts of formulae that people use to assess a goat's worth, but there is really no way to tell you how much you should pay for your goat(s). It is possible that you can purchase a nice goat inexpensively, but responsible breeders generally charge a price in line with what the goat is worth.

At the end of the day, you will be purchasing a goat because you want one and the one you buy will be the one that appeals to you most, for whatever reason. If your new goat falls short of your expectations you may not keep her long, but she will certainly provide a learning experience and you probably won't ever forget her.

IDEAL HOUSING AND FENCING

If you are new to keeping livestock animals, you might make the mistake of bringing home a couple and only then thinking about how you are going to house them; this is definitely putting the cart before the goat, as it were. Fortunately, most people wanting to raise goats already have facilities that, with a little tweaking, will serve as a shelter for them. If you are new to this, it would be a good idea to learn more about goats through reading and practical experience before building more than the simplest new facilities.

There are several different ideas about how small herds should be housed. Traditionally, they were individually penned. This had some advantages, which boiled down to the fact that they got individual attention and you knew that because it was just one goat that was eating the feed, you could ascertain that it was getting proper rations, even if that goat was at the bottom of the pecking order. The main disadvantage is that even though single accommodation eliminates bullying, it deprives these very social creatures of the close companionship of other members of the herd. It is also more labour intensive for you, the keeper.

Communal housing allows the normal herd structure to develop and operate. It is less labour intensive, but you must keep a watchful eye to determine that all your animals are happy and well-fed. This of course doesn't really apply if all you have are two does. Keep them together and they will be company for each other, although there may be a problem having two women living in the same house.

If separate housing is the route you want to go, you will need a minimum of 3 square metres (33 square feet) per animal. The pens should be wide enough for the goats to turn around in and square is the ideal shape. Larger breeds of goat will need more space as will your does when they are kidding. One of the disadvantages of separate penning is that every time you add a goat, you must also add a pen.

If your goats will be raised in what is sometimes called 'loose housing' — free to move about in a common pen, you must allow a minimum of 1.5 square metres (about 17 square feet) per animal, plus extra space for passageways and feeding stations. Again, if you have larger breeds, increase that figure and never put horned and hornless goats together because the horned ones will dominate and perhaps hurt the others during fights and completely monopolise the food.

Goats are not particularly house-proud. In fact, they don't much care whether they are living in a garage, shed, barn or an old chicken coop, which can all be adapted for the purpose. What is important is that the building should be dry and free from draughts, and you must provide plenty of dry, clean bedding. There should also be sufficient fresh air as poor ventilation will lead to respiratory problems. Wooden structures are easily adaptable, but some goats may chew them. Otherwise brick and stone are good building materials, and concrete floors are the easiest to clean.

If you are building from scratch, proper housing will protect your goats from the hardships of weather: heat, cold and rain. It should be easy for you to move around in, but should also ease the movement of the goats, who will eat, drink and be milked here; births will also take place in the building. Water and electrical connections are useful to have. The ceiling should ideally be at least 250 cm (8 feet) high. If you are using a very high building, you can add a loft in which you can store feed and bales of hay or straw.

Facilities for goats need not be either elaborate or expensive. You will want to keep them and their surroundings as hygienic and clean as possible. Plan living quarters that are easy to keep clean, pleasant for both you and your goats to be in, and this will certainly contribute to your goats' health and well-being. The design of your goat 'house' depends on the amount of land and outbuildings you have, your budget and your personal preferences. There is no best plan for everyone.

Whatever sort of housing you decide on, whether you are adapting or building, you will need to provide a large enough place for the goats to rest lying down, an eating area, a separate area in which to milk them, enough space for kids, plus a storage area to keep feed and bedding. In addition, you will need to ensure that your goats get enough fresh air and exercise. Housed goats need access to pasture or garden so they can graze. As they are browsers, you must deny them access to any poisonous shrubs, trees and plants, e.g., yew, rhododendron and laurel. You will also want to keep them from eating your roses!

Fencing is crucial and more difficult with goats than any other livestock animal. Goats don't like being fenced in, so whatever you dream up, if there is any way they can jump over, crawl under, squeeze through or try to destroy it, they will. Proper fencing will not only keep your goats from running away, it will protect them from stray dogs, foxes and other predators.

There are four ways to fence goats: chain link fencing, stock fencing, electric fencing, or a combination.

Chain link fencing is ideal for goats, but it is expensive, so unless you are fencing a rather small area, your budget may not extend to it.

Stock fencing is almost as good and is a cheaper alternative. It consists of 6mm ($1/4$ inch) welded steel rods, making it sturdy and ideal for goat pens. A height of 120 cm (4 feet) is usually sufficient. However, goats just love to rub themselves against this type of fencing, so you must check regularly to ensure that they have not broken any of the vertical wires. Stock fencing can be a problem with horned goats as they can get their heads stuck in it, especially as kids, but recent improvements feature panels with 10 cm (4 inch) spaces, which eliminates this problem.

Electric fencing is very successful with goats, but they must be trained to respect it. Once they learn what happens when they touch it, it is possible to fence even large areas at low cost. The only problem with this sort of fencing is that it must be kept free from vegetation to prevent fusing.

If the fence is against a bank or hedge, you may need combination fencing because goats will tend to stand on stock fencing to reach the vegetation. A single electric strand about 40 cm (16 inches) high and 30 cm (12 inches) from the fence should prevent this problem.

NUTRITION AND FEEDING

This is the most complicated part of raising goats and the goat owner's biggest expense. There is a lot of misinformation floating around regarding the feeding of goats. The average non-goat owner has been led to believe that goats will eat anything — including laundry hanging up on a clothesline — but they don't as a general rule.

Some of the things we feed goats aren't really all that good for them, complicated by the fact that opinion varies wildly about what we *should* be feeding them. Since even the experts can't offer really clear guidelines, you will have to separate the wheat from the chaff as it were and decide for yourself what is best for your goats.

As a beginner, this can be very confusing. If you grow hay and mix your own supplemental feed, you will not only need to know a good deal about nutrition, but a lot of science and maths. If you buy good hay and commercially prepared grain rations, and follow the directions on the label, your life as a goat keeper and the health of your goats will be much improved.

Feeding goats is very different from feeding cats, dogs or pet birds. Goats are ruminants (cud chewers), which affects their dietary needs. Goats are also productive animals, which puts additional strain on their bodies and requires extra nutrients.

The bulk of a goat's diet consists of forage: green plants and hay. But this doesn't mean that you can leave your goats in the pasture or garden to eat any old grass or plants and expect it to provide the nutrition your goats need (especially if you are raising dairy goats). Grass and hay do not provide all the vitamins and minerals a goat needs to be productive. The grain ration provides these.

Without getting too technical about it, an understanding of your goat's digestive system will help you to feed it properly. Like all true ruminants (cows, sheep, deer, bison, giraffes, etc.) they have what most people call 'four stomachs', but what is actually one four-chambered stomach consisting of the rumen, reticulum, omasum and abomasum (see diagram below).

THE GOAT'S DIGESTIVE SYSTEM
Including the ruminant's four-chambered stomach.

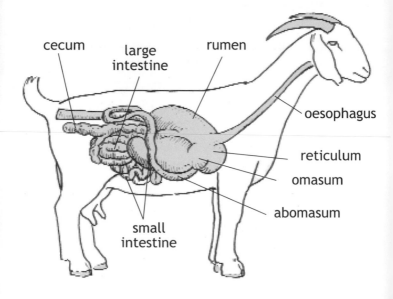

The rumen is the first and largest of the chambers. Essentially it is a large fermentation vat. When food is first consumed, it is mixed with saliva and enters the rumen, separating into layers of solids and liquids. Later on, when the goat is resting, it regurgitates a quantity of food, re-chews it more slowly, then swallows it again. During this, and subsequent chewings and swallowings, the food is mixed with more and more saliva, keeping the acidity/alkalinity at a healthy balance.

Once it is sufficiently liquefied, the chewed food exits the rumen and passes into the reticulum where fermentation continues (methane is produced continuously by bacteria and protozoa in the rumen and reticulum, the source of the goats' smelly belches), until it passes into the omasum.

The omasum is divided by long folds of tissue that resemble the pages of a book. These are covered with small, nipple-like protuberances called papillae that help decrease the size of feed particles, remove excess fluid and absorb any fatty acids that weren't absorbed in the rumen.

The last chamber, the abomasum, is considered the goat's 'true' stomach because this is where digestion occurs, much as it does in the stomachs of cats, dogs and humans.

Ruminants can be divided into those who are coarse feed eaters, munching grass and weeds from the ground, ingesting the largest amount possible, without being particularly selective. Cows and sheep fall into this category.

Tender feed eaters, like antelopes and gazelles, ingest smaller quantities of food, seeking out the most nourishing parts of the plant, such as young shoots, small weeds and blossoms in grass, weeds, bushes and trees.

Goats do not fall into either of these two categories. They are very adaptable feeders. The feeding behaviour of the goat has much to do with its original habitat — the mountains. In the summer, mountainous terrain provides an abundance of succulent plants, grass, trees and bushes. In the winter, there is very little available except for dried grass, withered plants, tree bark and the needles of conifers. The wild goat utilised the varied diet of summer by choosing the richest nutrients. In the winter, it had to make do with a much poorer selection of food. This explains the contradiction in the goat's reputation between being a picky eater on the one hand and eating anything in sight on the other.

In their ideal world, goats prefer to browse, nibbling at leaves of bushes, trees and weeds, rather than eat grass. They don't turn up their noses at grass, but like variety. These nibbling habits often get them into trouble if they manage to get into your vegetable garden, because they won't just eat a head of lettuce, then go onto another; it is more likely they will take a few bites of everything. This behaviour has given them the untrue reputation of being gluttonous.

Here are a few practical tips for feeding goats. They have been taken from an excellent booklet,

Feeding Goats, available from the British Goat Society, www.allgoats.com, which covers this subject in great depth, taking into account the sex, age and purpose of the goats you are keeping.

- The aim should be to keep every goat in good bodily condition all the year round.
- Good feeding can only be effective as part of a total package of good management, including adequate housing, exercise and health care, particularly the prevention and treatment of parasitic worm infestations.
- Food must be stored properly prior to feeding, to protect it from damp, contamination and vermin.
- Food must be hygienically presented to the herd with an understanding of goat behaviour so that each animal gets its share.
- Good hay is the single most important item in a goat's diet.
- At least half of the diet should consist of forage. Green food, concentrates, minerals, vitamins and water are also very important, and a balanced and adequate diet is crucial to success.
- Any change to the diet must be made gradually to enable the population of rumen bacteria to adjust.
- Kids must receive colostrum immediately after their birth, followed by a sufficient milk diet leading up to weaning.
- Drinking water must be clean, fresh and always available.

The following is a rough estimate of the amount of concentrates (oats, corn and goat mixes) to be fed. This quantity should be divided into two feeds a day. However, it must be stressed that the feeding of concentrates should always and only be a supplement to the feeding of good quality fibre in the form of hay and other forages.

Dairy goats
500 g (18 oz) plus about 200 g (7 oz) for each litre of milk produced per day.

Pregnant goats
Concentrates need to be fed in the last six weeks of gestation, starting from a small amount and increasing to about 1–1½ kg (2.2–3.3 lb) for a large dairy goat to 500 g (18 oz) for a fibre or meat goat and up to 200–300 g (7–11 oz) for a pygmy.

Young stock
From 200–600 g (7–21 oz) depending on size and time since weaning. Kids to be mated in their first year will need higher quantities compared with those who will not be mated until their second autumn. Such goatlings often do not need any concentrates in their second summer or they may get too fat.

Males
From 500 g–1½ kg (18 oz–3.3 lb) depending on size. Many males will starve themselves during the stud season, but will make up for it in the spring.

Remember that this is just a guide. *Feeding Goats* will give you a much fuller picture as will your vet and local feed supplier.

HEY! LET'S TALK ABOUT HAY

Since approximately 50 per cent of what your goat will eat is hay, you should have some knowledge of what exactly hay is and, since there are so many sorts, what kind of hay is best for goats.

The short answer is GOOD hay. Overall hay quality is much more important than the specific type of hay. Goats, being ruminants, thrive on forages. The rumen houses microbes that ultimately feed on these forages. These microbes allow ruminants to make use of plant materials that are indigestible by monogastric (single-stomached) animals such as humans. An average goat requires about 10–14 per cent crude protein and 60–65 per cent TDN (total digestible nutrients) on a dry matter basis in the total diet (combination of all hay, pasture and supplements eaten). There are many different species of grasses and edible pods that are regularly harvested as hay.

While some goat-owners may have a personal preference as to the type of hay that their goats receive, there is no one type of 'goat hay' that can, or even should be used. Any type of hay that is of good to excellent quality and is properly harvested and stored can be successfully fed to goats with correct management.

Hay is usually classified in the following manner:

Excellent hay
Alfalfa cut in late bud to early bloom; clover at 20

per cent bloom; grasses cut at the boot stage (when grass heads are still enclosed by the sheath of the uppermost leaf and no seed heads are showing). Hay is bright to medium green, leafy and free of dust, mustiness and mould. This quality of hay is high in protein, energy, minerals and carotene, but relatively low in fibre. This should be fed to goats in very small quantities, if at all, but it is ideal for kids, lactating does and other goats requiring palatable, high-energy forage.

Good hay

Legumes (lucerne or clover) cut at 50 per cent bloom; grass cut as it begins to head. This hay is reasonably soft, leafy, green and free of dust, mustiness and mould. Good hay is clean, smells pleasant, should have some flowers and not too many seeds. For goats, the presence of meadow plants will greatly increase its palatability. Legume hay is loved by goats and is higher in food value than grass hay. Unfortunately, it is difficult to find and is expensive.

Fair hay

Legumes (lucerne or clover) harvested at full bloom. This hay has a green or yellow tinge. It is stemmy and low in protein, energy, minerals and carotene and high in fibre. It may contain a moderate amount of dust, so don't feed it inside an enclosed barn. This hay is usable, but should be supplemented with grain and protein.

Poor hay
Anything cut after full bloom. It has a lot of stems, few leaves and is yellow or brown. It may be dusty, musty or mouldy and is not worth buying.

Straw (dried plant matter from cereals and peas) is not the same as hay. It is also quite liked by goats, but it is too low in food value for a highly productive goat. Straw is much better used as bedding than feed.

Much hay is ruined through improper storage. If you can, choose small bales stored indoors, avoiding bottom bales that might harbour mould and top bales that have been contaminated with bird or cat droppings.

Large bales kept under cover are a better buy than bales stored in fields, which, in areas of heavy rain or snowfall, can represent up to 35 per cent waste. If they are stored outside, the bales should be placed on pallets to keep them off the ground and covered with plastic after they are fully cured. Don't store bales close together (touching each other side by side). Instead, store in a line end to end. Also don't stack them. Both of these methods trap moisture between the bales, rendering them useless.

KEEPING YOUR GOATS HEALTHY

Goats are among the healthiest and hardiest of domestic animals. If you pay attention to proper feeding and management details, your goats should have very few health problems.

If your animals become ill, it's because of wrong diet, environment or perhaps even breeding. Treating the symptoms will help in the short haul, but unless the underlying causes are found and corrected, the problems will return. Some illnesses have a purpose. For instance, diarrhoea. This is fairly common in kids and can result from feeding too much milk, too cold milk or dirty utensils. In this case diarrhoea is the cure.

The best advice is to start with healthy stock, and manage them as carefully as you can. These are some very rudimentary guidelines:

HEALTHY GOAT	UNHEALTHY GOAT
Alert and curious	Dull and uninterested in its surroundings
Bright, clear eyes	Dull eyes. May have discharge in corners of eyes
Dry, cool noses with regular, unlaboured breathing	May have thick opaque white, yellow or green nasal discharge. May wheeze, cough or breathe unevenly

Clean, glossy hair coats	Dull, dry hair coats
Smooth skin free of vermin and eruptions	Skin may show evidence of parasites or skin disease
Moves freely and easily	Moves slowly, unevenly or with a limp
Average weight for breed and age	Underweight for breed or age, or skinny
Healthy appetite	Won't eat
Chews cud after eating	Doesn't chew cud
Firm droppings	May have diarrhoea
Clean tail and surrounding area	Tail area and hair on hind legs may be matted and dirty
Normal temperature (38.6°C—40.2°C) for adult goats. Kids may have slightly higher temperatures	Abnormally high or low temperature. Lower temperatures are usually more worrying than fevers

If you have any concerns about the health of your goats, your first source of information should be your vet (make sure you have one before you buy your first goat) or an experienced goat breeder.

There are some things that you can do to keep your goats as healthy as possible:

• Monitor them at least once a day to determine that they look healthy and uninjured. If you are unsure, call your vet.

• Maintain dry, clean surroundings for your goats. Provide adequate drainage in barns and housing areas. Regularly shovel manure out and offer draught-free shelter from the elements.

• Don't keep more goats than you have space for. Overcrowding leads to stress and manure build-up.

• Keep an eye out for accidents waiting to happen in the garden and pasture: protruding nails, sharp edges on buildings, fences that need repair, insect nests, etc. Don't let your goats climb onto stored hay — they can fall and injure themselves or even suffocate.

• Keep goats safe from predators by maintaining your fences and providing guardian animals for them if necessary.

• Try not to stress your goats when you are handling, transporting or weaning them.

• Assemble a first-aid kit. Ask your vet for advice regarding supplies you should keep on hand.

- Closely monitor pregnant does and be with them at kidding time. Learn how to assist if necessary. I have a friend who will leave a dinner party to be with his livestock when they are calving so that his elderly stockman doesn't have to be on duty at night.

- Choose proper goat feeds. If you don't know how to formulate your own feed, buy commercially prepared concentrates. Feed good quality hay. Make certain that timid goats are not being pushed away from feeders. Make all changes in feeds gradually, allowing your goats time to get used to the changes.

- Control rats or mice in feeding areas. Don't allow cats, dogs or poultry to defecate in hay or other feeds.

- Provide plenty of fresh, clean water. If you wouldn't drink it, neither should your goats.

- If you add any goats to your herd, quarantine them and thoroughly disinfect the area afterwards.

- Test all dead animals, including aborted foetuses, to determine the cause of death and ask your vet for details. Remove dead animals and placentas immediately. Properly dispose of them by burning, burial or composting.

- Vaccinate your goats against enterotoxaemia and tetanus. To cover as many types of enterotoxaemia as possible, use a four-in-one vaccine for sheep. Discuss a vaccination programme with your vet and add any other immunisations recommended for goats raised in your area.

- Have your goats tested for CAE (*Caprine Arthritis Encephalitis*): an incurable virus which fortunately is not too common in the UK.

- Trim hooves on a regular basis to maintain soundness and prevent hoof deformities.

WHEN YOUR GOATS ARE UNWELL

Even with the best care and management, goats do get ill. There are so many possible diseases and ailments that it doesn't make any sense for a person with a few goats to even try to be familiar with them all. It is also easy for an amateur to misdiagnose animal illnesses. So if you have a sick goat, call your vet.

Having said that, there are a few common ailments that you should know about.

INTERNAL PARASITES (WORMS)

'Worms' of various sorts are the most widespread and serious threat to a goat's well-being, the most common ones being roundworm, tapeworm and liver fluke, but only if they are present in large quantities.

A small number of roundworms will do your goats no harm; it is just about impossible to have a goat that doesn't have some. However, parasitic worms multiply rapidly and if they are not dealt with, they will cause anaemia and could be fatal.

The best method of dealing with potential or real problems with parasites consists of two simple steps — regular, close visual inspections of your goats, and periodic faecal exams so that your vet can determine which parasites are present and which products to use to combat them.

To inspect your goats, you should pay attention to its mucous membranes, gums and eyes. The whites of the eyes should not be white, but pink or red. If they are white, grey or pale pink, this is an indication of anaemia and the likely cause is worms.

If you worm your goats regularly with the same product, the parasites could build up a resistance to the medication, so it is suggested that you change to a different type of wormer every year. Because most wormers are not specifically licensed for use in milking goats in the UK, there is a minimum milk withholding time before the milk can be used for human consumption, of seven days for all the wormers currently on sale. Some vets think the withdrawal time for dairy goats ought to be doubled. The withdrawal time for meat by law is 28 days.

Books and breeders suggest worming goats on a schedule, but you can also ask your vet to inspect them for parasites and if they need to be wormed. This approach is not only cheaper in the long run; it is easier on both you and the goats.

When you do have to use a wormer, it can be administered as a drench, an injection or in the goats' food. This last method sounds easiest, but how do you ensure that the goats are actually ingesting it? They are very cunning about moving their food around to avoid it. Drenching is the most common technique, usually applied by syringe, squirting the medication down the goat's throat. Watching to see how it is done is much simpler than trying to describe it.

Coccidiosis should be mentioned in any discussion about parasites. This disease is caused by microscopic protozoa (*coccidia*) found in the cells of the intestinal lining. Most adult goats carry a small population of coccidia, but it will not do them any harm. The greatest danger is to kids one to four months old. All buildings housing kids must be thoroughly cleaned at the start of each kidding season and bedding must be frequently changed. Food, water and milk containers should also be thoroughly cleaned. The most common symptom of coccidiosis is diarrhoea, although you might also notice that the kid seems weak. Prevention is possible by adding sulfonamide drugs to the feed. Wormers are completely useless in treating this disease.

EXTERNAL PARASITES

No matter how well kept they are, all goats should be checked for lice. They can cause tremendous irritation to your goats, damage the skin and hair and cause anaemia. Suspect lice if your goat is abnormally fidgety, has started to nibble itself and has a dull, scruffy coat. Lice can be seen with the naked eye. Pour-on products have been used with success, but there are no licensed products for use on milking animals. Discuss treatment with your vet.

Mites are responsible for different types of mange, which is indicated by flaky 'dandruff' on the skin. It usually shows up as bald, irritated patches. Some mange can be very difficult to eliminate. It can be treated with a variety of medications available from vets, who are best qualified to determine which mite needs to be addressed and what the proper treatment should be. Ringworm is another problem that can look like mange, but this is actually a fungus that shows up as round bald patches.

Blowflies are a much bigger problem with sheep than with goats. They are usually attracted to dirt and wounds, which should be sprayed with an antibiotic that has a fly deterrent in it.

SCRAPIE

Scrapie is a fatal brain disease affecting sheep and goats. The disease develops due to changes in a protein present in the brain known as prion protein. By law, any animals suspected of having scrapie must be reported to your local Animal Health Divisional Office (ADHO). An excellent booklet, *Scrapie — Advisory Notes for Farmers* can be downloaded from this Defra site www.defra.gov.uk/animalh/bse/othertses/ scrapie/adv-note.pdf.
This rather complicated subject is not suitable for discussion in a book of this nature.

MASTITIS

Mastitis is an inflammation of the mammary gland (udder), usually caused by an infection. Symptoms are a hot, hard, tender udder; milk may be stringy, strange-tasting or bloody. Other symptoms may be reluctance to be milked, not wanting to let kids suckle, or a sudden drop in milk yield. It is usually a relatively minor problem, but some cases may be fatal.

Mastitis can occur in any milking goat, not just dairy goats. Particular attention should be paid when kids do not look satisfied. The dam may appear quite normal, but she also may look off-colour.

Mastitis can be caused by injury to the udder, poor milking techniques, or by transference by one milker from one animal to another. Hand milkers should wash their hands between each animal and udders and teats should be washed and dried before milking. Teat dips have been successful in controlling this disease in cattle, but they must be diluted for goats.

There is a widespread belief that goats must be milked at 12-hour intervals, but studies have proved that goats milked at intervals of eight or 16 hours produced as much as those milked at 12, with no increase of mastitis.

KETOSIS

Ketosis includes pregnancy disease, acetonaemia and others. They are metabolic diseases caused by poor nutrition before and after birthing. If a goat's demand for high energy food is not met, she will feed on herself internally, using up her own body reserves which produces toxic ketones in the body. If spotted early, the disease can be treated, but if ignored, it can be fatal. Symptoms include a lack of appetite and listlessness. It is most likely to affect fat does, especially those that get little exercise. Some goats will also have a distinct 'pear drop' (acetone) smell to their breath. Treatment includes administering 180–240 ml (6–8 fl oz) of propylene glycol orally twice a day for no longer than two days. In an emergency you can dose 15 ml (1 tablespoon) sodium bicarbonate in 120 ml (4 fl oz) water, followed by 250 g (9 oz) honey or molasses.

This summarises most of the things that can make your goat unwell. But since you are probably an overanxious 'parent' at this stage in your goat keeping, it is best to let your vet diagnose whether your goats really have a health problem.

GROOMING YOUR GOATS

Goats aren't particularly high maintenance animals, but that doesn't mean they don't require any care. A goat owner will quickly learn how to clip and trim hooves, disbud and tattoo.

The most important grooming item is hoof care.

HOOF TRIMMING

The horny outside layer of the goat's hoof grows like a human's fingernails and must be trimmed periodically or your goat can become lame. If your goats are not on a hard surface, this will need doing every month. You can increase the time between trimmings by placing rough breeze blocks in the garden or pasture with the holes turned to the side. Your goats will love climbing on them and the abrasive surface will help minimise your trimming duties.

How to trim hooves correctly will need to be shown to you by an experienced goat keeper so that you can see what needs to be done. But the rudiments of this task are fairly simple. You will need goat hoof clippers and a very sharp knife or a surform (a small woodworker's plane with blades). A stiff brush and pair of heavy work gloves are also useful.

To be able to do this properly, the goat needs to be in a comfortable position. Restrain the goat by haltering or collaring and secure it next to a wall. Beginning with a front leg, lift the leg as little as possible, flexing it back with the hoof facing up.

You must do the bending or you will make the goat uncomfortable. Don't twist it out to the side because it will hurt and your goat may kick. If the hoof is dirty, scrub it with a brush.

Using the point of the clippers, dig out any dirt stuck in the hoof. Pare off the overgrown wall of the hoof (the hard outside section) until it is even with the sole all the way round. Trim away any rotted pockets between the sole and the hoof wall. Trim the toe so it is even with the sole and snip off any excess growth between the two heel areas. Once this is done, the softer, more sensitive inner section should be pared level with a very sharp knife or a surform. Trim very slowly, a sliver at a time, stopping when the sole starts to show a very gentle shade of pink. If you go any further, you may cause bleeding. If this happens (and it will from time to time), don't panic. Simply place the foot on a firm surface so there is no pressure on it and staunch the blood with flour or cornflour. When it stops bleeding, apply an antibiotic spray as a precaution. The trimmed hooves should be perfectly level and look nice and neat.

If you start trimming when your goats are young, they will become accustomed to the procedure. As long as the goat is comfortable, do not let go if it objects because it will try to get you to stop. Just remember that a neglected and overgrown foot requires much more work and probably the assistance of an experienced goat keeper.

DISBUDDING

Disbudding is the term used for the removal of the horn buds before they have grown. With most kids this has to be done between the ages of two days and two weeks. There are many arguments for and against.

The keepers who think horns should be kept believe:

- they are protection against dogs and other predators
- they help to cool the goat
- they are natural — a goat doesn't really look like a goat without them
- disbudding is a ghastly procedure

Those who believe in disbudding think:

- horns are dangerous to other goats and people, especially children
- if you are using a manger to feed your goats, it is impossible to build one to accommodate horns
- horns aren't that much protection against dogs or other predators

One thing that everyone agrees on it that it is better to disbud than de-horn, which can be painful and even dangerous to the goat. Most vets do not like de-horning as it is a major operation and if not done properly can cause large holes in the head which will need careful aftercare.

As both disbudding and de-horning have to be done under anaesthesia, they can only be performed by a vet. Under no circumstances should you let a farmer do it since the disbudding of kids is very different from the disbudding of calves.

If your male kids are being kept entirely for stud, it is a good idea to ask your vet to cauterise the scent glands when he does the disbudding. While this will not keep your male from smelling, it can reduce the odour.

IDENTIFYING YOUR GOATS — TAGGING AND TATTOOING

All goats must be individually identified with a UK tag within nine months of birth (for extensively reared animals — less goats on larger acreage) or six months of birth (for intensively reared animals — more goats on smaller acreage) or before they leave the holding on which they were born, whichever happens first.

The law allows for sheep and goats to be marked by either an ear tag or a tattoo. It is important that tagging or tattooing is carried out correctly to ensure the welfare of your animals. Taking care will also minimise ear tag losses and associated problems. Follow these guidelines carefully to ensure that the ear tag or tattoo is correctly applied and to avoid unnecessary pain or distress to your animals.

Tattooing is the method often favoured for goats (some of which have the habit of chewing ear tags!). The tattoo should be easily read on animals with little skin pigmentation. For reading marks in black ears, it is often helpful to apply an electric torch directly to the back of the animal's ear and read the mark with the aid of the light shining through the ear. Remember that the tattoo cannot be read until some days after applying the ink. You should tattoo well in advance of the need for reading the mark (e.g., at a sale).

Tattooing requires more patience than tagging. It also has more potential (than most current designs of ear tag) for transmission of disease between animals.

- Make sure that your operator is properly trained and competent.

- After loading the tattoo pliers with the relevant characters, be sure to check the tattoo on clean, thick paper or cardboard before applying to your animal. Replace characters that are broken or worn immediately.

- Hold the animal's head to prevent jerking during tattooing.

- Cleanse the area to be tattooed with surgical or methylated spirit to remove dirt, grease and wax. Allow the area to dry. Rub in ink with a clean ball of cotton wool. The use of tattoo ink, preferably green rather than black, is critical in getting a legible and permanent tattoo.

- Place the ear between the jaws of the tattoo pliers. Make sure that the characters are parallel to and between veins and cartilage. Make the imprint quickly and firmly. Use sufficient pressure that the skin is pierced but does not bleed profusely. Immediately apply more ink and rub vigorously and continuously for at least 15 seconds to ensure penetration.

- Do not disturb the area until the healing process is complete, which may be from five to 21 days.

It is imperative to clean the tattooing equipment thoroughly between each use as it is likely to become contaminated with blood and can lead to the transmission of disease. When making the decision to tattoo, instead of applying ear tags, you should be aware that the risk of disease transmission cannot be completely removed, even by apparently thorough cleansing and disinfection of equipment.

Before commencing a new session of ear tattooing, and before tattooing each animal, you are recommended to follow the guidance below. However, you must appreciate that this action does not eliminate the risk of disease transmission:

- Remove any debris, i.e. skin, hair, blood and ink paste, from the pliers and characters.

- Wash the applicator and characters in clean, preferably running, cold water and carefully dry with a clean cloth.

- The tattoo applicator and characters should then be soaked in disinfectant in the correct dilution for at least one minute.

- Discard characters that are broken or worn; the sponge rubber pad should be replaced when it begins to lose its elasticity.

- The animals should be checked initially for signs of excessive bleeding and for the next few days for signs of local infection. Where problems are evident, a veterinarian should be consulted.

If you need any further information about ear tagging or tattooing of sheep and goats, please contact your local Animal Health Divisional Office (AHDO).

BREEDING AND KIDDING

It goes without saying that to get milk, you must breed your goats in order to produce kids. The 150 days gestation period between mating and kidding is a very important one for the doe and for the first time goat keeper; it is a time filled with anxiety.

MATING

Like most other animals, goats are fertile for relatively short periods. Unlike cows, pigs and rabbits, which come into heat year round, goats and sheep generally do so only in the autumn and early winter, and kid in the spring.

Goats may only be mated when they are 'in season', which may be anything from 12—60 hours with a repeat cycle of 21 days, although a few goats may have a slightly shorter or longer cycle.

Doelings are sexually mature from the age of three or four months, but they should not be bred this early. Well-developed and healthy kids can be bred at seven or eight months when they weigh about 36 kg (80 lb), which means that they will kid at about one year. Breeding too early will adversely affect their growth and milk production; breeding too late will not contribute to their well-being either. It is believed that one-year-old does who kid produce more milk in a lifetime than those that are 'held over'. With proper nutrition they will produce healthy kids and keep growing themselves.

A goat in season may show any of the following signs: nervous bleating for the male; increased tail wagging; slightly swollen vulva, sometimes with a clear discharge which might show as wetness on the bottom of the tail; trying to mount other goats; loss of appetite and a drop in milk production. If a buck is nearby, there will be no doubt because she will moon around the buck acting like a lovesick teenager!

If there is no buck in the immediate vicinity, you could try the 'billy rag' trick. Rub a clean rag over the smelliest parts of a male goat and put it into a self-seal plastic bag. If you suspect your doe is in heat, give her a whiff of the rag. If she is interested, she will probably wag her tail and maybe push her back up slightly. But you can't get your doe pregnant with tinned buck aroma, so you will have to find a buck to take her to. If you wish to mate your doe and you get to the end of December without her being in season, you will need to consult your vet.

If you have both male and female goats and your does are in season, you could just let them get on with it, but if you want a specific male to be used or if any of your goats is horned, the mating will need to be supervised.

To determine whether the mating was successful, wait 21 days to see if your doe comes into season again — also watch for signs at 42 days. If this doesn't happen you can assume she is in kid.

Pregnancy is easiest to diagnose in a milk goat as a sample of her milk can be sent off to be tested for the presence of oestrogen sulphate. This test has a high degree of accuracy. For a non-milk goat, an ultrasonic scanner can be used. In any event, diagnosis can be made after 35 days. It is also possible to determine the number of babies with ultrasound, but this has a lower rate of accuracy. If a doe is serviced and still comes back in heat, she might not have been bred at the most opportune time. Perhaps one more try will do the trick.

GESTATION

Once your doe is pregnant, you will need to make some changes in her diet. A fibrous diet with rather low protein is ideal for the first three months when the kids are developing slowly. Most foetus growth is in the last eight weeks. During this period the feed needs to be changed gradually; not only because two-thirds of the kids' growth is taking place, but because the doe has to build up her own reserves. There is a definite need for minerals and vitamins, especially calcium, iodine and vitamins A and D. Fibre, such as bran, will also be required, as will molasses to supply iron. Does fed ample molasses during gestation are less likely to encounter ketosis. It also has a slight laxative effect, which is desirable at this stage.

PARTURITION — GIVING BIRTH

Birth is a miracle that fills you with wonder, excitement and joy. It doesn't matter whether you witness it in humans or in the animal world — it is really awesome. There have been many people who haven't cared about goats at all until they saw newborn kids finding their feet — and then it was a case of love at first sight.

First time goat keepers also experience apprehension. Perhaps they have read too much about what could go wrong and worry that it will. But goats have been having kids all by themselves for thousands of years. Problems are possible, but 95 per cent of the time they will not happen. It is best to be there when it happens even if it just puts your mind at rest.

A wild goat on a mountain will know exactly what to do and where to do it, but since you are controlling your goat's environment, it is preferable for you to have some idea of when the birth is imminent and to make some preparations.

The first kidder tends to show less sign of pinkness around the vulva than the doe that has already kidded, but about three and a half to four months into the gestation, the doe should start to produce a small udder. Another sign to look for, although this will not be as obvious in a new mother, is 'ridging up'. This is where the spine from the hips to the tail appears to rise up as the bones loosen in preparation for birth. When the process is nearly complete you can almost get your fingers around the spine near the base of the tail. As the birth approaches, you should ensure that you have a few minimal kidding supplies to hand: a small, clean water pail, chopped hay for bedding, baby bottles and teats and frozen colostrum (just in case you need it).

When the time comes, some goats will kid within a couple of hours; others will be out of sorts and fidgety for days beforehand.

There are some typical signs of early labour, which may not occur in this order:

- Appears restless, shies away from other goats
- Eyes glossy or luminous; dreamy-eyed
- Pays attention to her sides and smells the ground
- Paws at bedding
- Looks behind her and 'talks' to her babies
- Talks to you a lot as if she is telling you she is getting ready. She is, so listen
- Urinates frequently, but not much at a time
- Lays down and gets up more than usual and seems more fidgety
- Udder begins to fill, looks tight and shiny and teats get full
- Vulva becomes flabby, then looks flat and the opening looks longer
- White discharge (may not happen), changing to albumin-looking discharge which may have some blood streaks

The doe should have her own pen for kidding that you have prepared for her. It should be as antiseptic as possible and thickly bedded with fresh, clean chopped straw. Do not leave water in the kidding pen. It can be dangerous and the doe wouldn't be interested in it anyway.

Eventually she will lie down on her side and start to strain, accompanied by frequent changes in position. Then the serious straining will start. Do not be alarmed when she starts to scream, usually very loudly. Most goats are very vocal — this is quite normal. Once this has started, the kids should be born within 20 minutes or so. If nothing happens, call the vet at this point.

During the normal kidding process, the first thing you will see is a balloon-like membrane, inside of which you will see two small feet, followed by a nose and then the head. It will take the greatest effort to get the head and shoulders out, especially in the first kidder.

If another five minutes passes and you don't see anything more happening, you can assist. Scrub your hands, apply Vaseline around the edge of the vulva and with one hand maintain a slight outward and downward pressure on the kid's legs. With the other hand, gently run your finger (make sure you have short, clipped fingernails) around the edge of the vulva to help stretch it. You will find that in the vast majority of cases, your doe will require no assistance from you at all, but again, if you see any other presentation than two front feet and a nose, call for assistance.

Twins are the norm, but triplets are not uncommon, and some breeds of goats have even more kids. After the first kid is born, make sure that it is not liable to be trod on. When the next one arrives, place it next to the first and make sure the mother attends to both. The dam will lick the kids, which stimulates them and helps them to dry out.

They will probably be on their feet within ten minutes or so and will be hungry, so help them to find the teats if necessary because the sooner the kid receives its first feed of colostrum, the better.

How do you know when the goat has finished kidding? Usually, the afterbirths will not be produced until all the kids have been born. Mama will also appear more comfortable, although there will probably be some straining to produce the afterbirth. Afterbirths are best removed after they are detached, but there will be no harm done if your doe eats hers. At this point she will probably appreciate a drink of molasses water or oat water.

Of course, you may never get to see the birth. You may have miscalculated, forgotten to write down the birthdates, or the 150 days may be 145 or 155. So the first thing you might see as you are going about your normal morning chores is a couple of dry, vigorous, playful kids in the pen with their new mother!

FEEDING THE DAM AFTER BIRTH

During the first week after birth, feed the dam cautiously. Overfeeding high value concentrates will produce a sudden flush of milk and could lead to problems such as milk fever. But to start with, give her plenty of good quality hay and perhaps a reduced ration of oats. Over the next week or two, you can probably reintroduce her to her normal ration in both quantity and quality. You might want to discuss her nutritional needs with an experienced goat keeper.

During the first few days after birth, feel the dam's udder often. It is possible that she may be overstocked with milk. In that event, remove about half of it from each side, but don't milk her completely. It is always a good idea to take some colostrum from the first goat to kid and freeze it in 100 g (3⅓ fl oz) portions in case of problems with later kiddings. Colostrum can be stored in the freezer for up to two years.

Regardless of whether the kids will be reared separately, it is a good idea to leave them with their dam for the first four days so that they have sufficient colostrum. They must have colostrum during the first six hours of their lives when the benefits of it are most easily absorbed.

KID REARING

Although baby goats are very appealing, you may find you have a surplus. So first you have to decide which ones to keep. Many people don't wish to raise buck kids. You then have the choice of rearing them for meat, giving them away after they have been weaned or humanely disposing of them.

Once you decide, you have three other choices to make: leave the dam to raise her own kids, which is common with fibre, meat and pet goats; leave the kids on the dam, but bottle feed some of the time (this works for milk goats); or bottle feed all of the time if you only have a small number of goat kids.

If you choose to go the natural route, most female goats will be able to rear two kids if they are in good physical condition. If there are triplets or quads involved, there may be problems with fibre or meat goats who are unlikely to have enough milk, so it may be necessary to remove one or two and bottle feed them. This should be done within the first few days, as it is difficult to get a kid who has suckled its dam to become used to an artificial teat. If the dam has produced only one kid, you must make sure that she doesn't get overstocked. A dairy goat with a singleton may regularly produce too much milk and will need daily milking.

Naturally reared kids will normally be weaned from about five to six months. You must be vigilant until then to make certain that the kids are getting enough nourishment.

The system of bottle-feeding part of the time is ideal for the goat keepers who want milk for their own use, but do not want to spend all of their time bottle feeding. The idea is to have a kid who will suckle its dam part of the time and take milk from a bottle as well. To achieve this, you separate the kids from their mother at four days, but they should still be able to see and touch each other (a sheet of welded wire mesh will suit this purpose). You can then bottle feed the kid four times a day for a week until it accepts the teat easily, then you can put it back with the dam. At the age of one month, you can separate the kids at night, take the majority of the morning milk for your use and put the kids back with their mother during the day. This method is useful if you have one kid you want to keep. If there are triplets or quads and the dam cannot feed them all, you can give additional bottle milk to the kids using this method.

Bottle feeding allows you to have complete control over the kids' nutrition. You can also keep precise records of what the dam is producing and feed her accordingly. The disadvantage is that it is very time consuming, but, if you have the time, it is a very pleasant occupation and allows early bonding between you and the kids.

In the beginning all young animals need to be fed little and often. This can be as often as five or six times a day. After the first week, you can decrease this to four feeds as long as the kid is drinking sufficient milk at each feed. After a month, the quantity will vary according to the breed with the heavier breeds taking about two litres a day and the pygmy goats less than a litre. Feed on demand, but watch that the kids aren't getting too fat. If you see this happening, put them on a reduced milk diet!

If you have had human children, you know how restricting it can be to have babies and how much work it is to continually sterilise bottles and teats. But the joys of this may compensate, because you will have very friendly, affectionate kids and goats.

Kids who are bottle fed are normally weaned at four to six months, depending on their growth progress. Gradually reduce the frequency and quantity of feeds and encourage your kids to eat good hay and concentrates.

TEENAGED GOATLINGS

A goatling is a female goat, over one year and under two years old, who has not yet borne a kid. In smallholdings in Britain it has been a tradition not to mate female goats until their second autumn when they are about 18 months old. It is believed that this practice helps produce larger, more productive goats. One disadvantage of this system is that goatlings tend to become overweight. You must guard against this, for your goats' health and because it is difficult to get fat goats into kid.

MALE GOATS

Let us not forget that male goats are necessary for the procreation of the next generation, but they are not easy to keep, and if you are thinking of keeping one as a stud you need to separate him from the females when he is quite young as he will make quite a pest of himself, and during the mating season will smell very strongly.

PROPER MILKING TECHNIQUES

One of the main reasons for keeping goats is to have milk that is better than any found in the shops.

If you intend to sell any milk at all for human consumption, you have to be registered and comply with tests on water and milk, as well as having all your buildings meet the standards of relevant regulations. This is generally beyond the scope of most small goat keepers.

If you just want to provide milk for your household and for animal consumption, few regulations apply. However, you still need to ensure that the milk is as clean as possible. Therefore, in an ideal world you would have a separate dairy to milk the goats in and a means of filtering and cooking the milk immediately after milking. All equipment used will have to be carefully disinfected twice a day after each milking. A booklet, *Easy Dairying*, published by the British Goat Society, offers very good advice.

Milking equipment can be very simple or very elaborate (and very expensive). At the simple end, you could have a bowl and strainer from your kitchen and store the milk in the refrigerator, but if you are planning on milking 730 times a year for the foreseeable future, you might at least want to invest in a milking pail, strainer, disposable filters, churn, strip cup, udder washing supplies and milking stool, which can be easily made from hardwood or bought ready-made.

The goats supplying the milk must be healthy and in good condition. The milking area should be clean and free of flies, dust and strong odours, away from the housing area. The floor and walls should have a clean, hard, washable surface and should be washed down after each milking. This will help to keep the dust down.

The hairs on the udder, flanks and hind legs of the goat should be trimmed and kept short. Brushing the goat before bringing her into the milking area will also help to keep the milk free of hair, dust and dung. The udder and teats should be washed with an udder wipe or a disposable cloth dipped into disinfectant solution and wrung out, then dried.

The foremilk: two or three squirts from each teat should be drawn into a strip cup, examined for clots and then discarded. The foremilk is likely to contain a heavy count of bacteria, which have gained access through the teat opening. If this foremilk does contain any clots, flakes, or is stringy, the goat probably has mastitis and should be milked separately, with the milk discarded. Strip cups have a black screen which makes these abnormalities more apparent.

The milker should wear a clean overall and head covering kept just for this purpose. Hands should be washed and dried with antibiotic soap before starting, between milking each goat and after handling any suspected sick animal.

Milking should be carried out as hygienically and quickly as possible. The milk from each goat should be strained through a filter into a churn or other suitable container. If the milk is not to be used immediately, it must be cooled to a temperature as close to 5°C (41°F) as soon as possible. Bacteria double in number every 20 minutes if the temperature exceeds 12°C (53°F).

When a churn is used and the mains water is not cold enough, put the churn into a larger container with a block of ice and fill with water. An ice block can be made by filling a 5-litre plastic container with water and freezing. Re-freeze after use.

Goat's milk can be frozen very successfully because of the small size of the fat globules.

CLEANING AND DISINFECTING UTENSILS

All equipment used for milking must be capable of being thoroughly cleaned and disinfected. Where possible, stainless steel is the ideal material – plastic cannot be cleaned thoroughly enough and aluminium becomes pitted.

The strainer should be the type used with a disposable filter pad: the pad is placed between two perforated metal discs and clipped into place. For very small milk production a fine mesh kitchen sieve will be sufficient.

This is the procedure:

- All utensils should be rinsed thoroughly with cold water immediately after use. This is very important since milk is very difficult to remove once it has dried. Do not use hot water as it will coagulate and stick to the surfaces of the utensils.

- Then scrub the utensils in hot, soapy water with the recommended amount of a suitable dairy detergent.

- Disinfect the equipment using either a suitable chlorine or iodine-based dairy chemical disinfectant, following the manufacturer's instructions exactly, invert on a rack and air-dry. Do not dry with a towel.

- Wooden equipment should have boiling water poured over after it has been cleaned. It must be made of hardwood.

- For extra insurance against bacterial contamination, just before using the equipment again, rinse with a very small amount of chlorine bleach (diluted 10:1) then rinse with boiling water.

Perhaps this sounds a bit over the top to you. You won't die from drinking milk that wasn't produced using strict laboratory methods, but if you want to do the best job, you know that you won't be doing it with soapy dishwater, a sponge and a tea towel. If you ever encounter milk that tastes a bit 'off', your milk handling and equipment cleaning procedures should be the first things to examine.

Now you are ready to learn about milking.

Milking looks very easy until you try it! It will be easy the more you practise. You will be glad you have a milking stool, as it is far more comfortable than squatting. Position yourself at the goat's side, facing the rear. Goats can be milked from either side, but if you are right-handed, the right side will be easier for you.

- The first step is washing the udder as described above. Dry the udder and your hands with kitchen paper, using a fresh sheet for each goat.

- Grasp the teat with your thumb and forefinger so the milk flows out of the teat, not back into the udder.

- Gently, but firmly, press the teat with your middle finger, forcing the milk down further. Close all your fingers around the teat using a steady pressure, and the milk should start to squirt out. Direct the first two or three squirts into your strip cup and discard as they will be high in bacteria.

- Then start milking into your pail, using first one hand on one teat and the other hand on the other teat. With a little practise you will develop a steady rhythm.

- Keep going until the milk flow ceases, then massage the udder as the kids do when they are nursing and you will get a few more squirts. This is important because not only does the last milk contain the most butterfat, but also if you don't get as much milk as possible, the goat will stop producing all she is capable of.

- The final step is stripping. You never get all the milk, but the last few drops can be extracted in this way. Take the teat between your thumb and first finger. Squeeze gently down the length of the teat once or twice, but avoid vigorous movement to prevent injury.

WHAT ABOUT NON-DAIRY GOATS?

Most of the emphasis in this book has been focused on dairy goats because this is the purpose for which most British goats are kept traditionally.

There is a bit of a sea change though. People wanting more exotic pets than cats, dogs and rabbits have brought some of it about, but there are other influences as well.

MEAT

Many of us are worried about our economic recession, the cost of food and how this is going to impact on us in the future. So we are laying plans to become more self-sustainable. We have also travelled to locations where eating goat meat is part of the culture. We have tasted it, and we like it! Add this to the fact that we have become a multi-ethnic country and the desire for goat products has increased in leaps and bounds. Celebrity chefs have also got into the act, cooking goat curries and the like. If you read my *Aloe Vera* book, you might remember that my sister lives in the Caribbean. She has kindly contributed her recipe for a goat curry she makes frequently for family and friends. You will find it on page 143.

FIBRE

Some people keep goats for their fleece. Angora goats must be shorn twice a year. The mohair is usually taken when the fibre is 9—15 cm (3½— 6 inches) long, just before kidding and in the autumn. Cashmere is combed out when it is shed in the spring. This purpose for keeping goats is not particularly popular in this country except amongst the really self-sufficient who spin, weave and knit their own clothing.

PETS

As I mentioned earlier, pygmy goats are becoming popular as pets as their curious, friendly nature makes them good companions. Unless you are prepared to nurture at least two, don't even consider it.

A decent amount of space is also necessary (a large garden or pasture), so they are best suited for rural areas on farms or smallholdings. If you live in a town or a city, local bylaws may prevent you from keeping goats as they might be classed as an agricultural species.

You must also be prepared for the commitment to having goats. They do need attention like any other pet, but additionally, you need to consider who can look after them when you go on holiday.

WHERE TO FIND RESCUE GOATS

There are many places in the UK to find rescue, re-homed goats. I have listed a few here by area, which are all correct at the time of writing. Obviously there may not always be goats available to adopt.

Cumbria
Animals Unlimited
Tel: 07764 352835

Cheshire
The Goat Sanctuary, Alderley Edge
Tel: 01565 873820
Web: www.thegoatsanctuary.org

Wettenhall Animal Rescue & Sanctuary, Winsford
Tel: 01270 528960

Devon
Firsland Animal Sanctuary, Daccombe
Tel: 01803 326954

Rainbow Valley Sanctuary, Ipplepen, nr Newton Abbot
Tel: 01803 814212
Web: www.rainbowvalleysanctuary.org.uk

East Midlands
East Midlands Open Rescue
Tel: 07988 724773
Web: www.openrescue.weebly.com

Essex
Remus Memorial Horse Sanctuary, Buttsbury
Tel: 01277 356191
Web: www.remussanctuary.org

Hopefield Animal Sanctuary, Brentwood
Tel: 01277 201110
Web: www.hopefield.org.uk

Hertfordshire
Farm Animal Rescue Sanctuary
Tel: 01784 461360

Kent
The Retreat Animal Rescue, Swanley
Tel: 01322 614247
Web: www.retreatanimalrescue.org

Friend Farmed Animal Rescue, Tonbridge
Tel: 01622 871617
Web www.friendsanimalrescue.org.uk

Leicestershire
Field Farm Animal Sanctuary, Loughborough
Tel: 01509 852702

Manor Farm Animal Centre and Donkey Sanctuary,
Loughborough Tel: 01509 852525
Web: www.manorfarm.info

Norfolk
Hillside Animal Sanctuary, Norwich
Tel: 01603 736200
Web: www.hillside.org.uk

Northamptonshire
Brook Farm Animal Sanctuary, Raunds
Tel: 07758 728265   Web: www.brook-farm.org.uk

West Midlands
Green Meadow Animal Sanctuary, Pattingham
Tel: 01902 701743

Surrey
Springflower Animal Sanctuary, Guildford
Tel: 07909 563809
Web: www.springfloweranimals.com

Warwickshire
Farm Animal Rescue Sanctuary, Wolverton,
nr Stratford-upon-Avon
Web: www.farmanimalrescue.org.uk

West Sussex
Animaline Sanctuary, Haywards Heath
Tel: 01342 810596
Web: www.carlalane.com/animaline

Paws Animal Sanctuary, Worthing
Tel: 01903 872734
Web: www.pawsanimalsanctuaryfindon.co.uk

Foxhollow Animal Sanctuary, Chichester
Tel: 07786 404602 or 07785 947829

Wiltshire
Abbey View Alpacas, Malmesbury
Tel: 01666 823124
Web: www.abbeyviewalpacas.com

SCOTLAND

Aberdeenshire
The New Arc (North East Wildlife & Animal Rescue), Ellon
Tel: 0796 2253867
Web: www.thenewarc.org

The Fernwood Trust, Peterhead
Tel: 08448 843 423
Web: www.fernwoodtrust.org

Dumfriesshire
Mossburn Animal Rescue Centre, Lockerbie
Tel: 01387 811288
Web: www.mossburn.org

Grampian
Willows Animal Sanctuary, Fraserburgh
Tel: 01771 653112
Web: www.willowsanimals.com

WALES

Trallwm Farm, Carmarthen
Tel: 08712 300873
Web: www.trallwmfarm.co.uk

Capricorn Animal Rescue, Clwyd
Tel: 01244 547938

All Creatures Great and Small, Cwmbran, Gwent
Tel: 01633 866144
Web: www.allcreaturesgreatandsmall.org.uk

HUMANE SLAUGHTER

While death is always an unpleasant subject, it is a necessary one. In terms of goat keeping, we need to think of it on two levels: if you are keeping meat goats, there comes a time when they must provide food. And if you are keeping any kind of goats, if your goat is ill and all else fails, you also have to consider humane slaughter.

Cruelty to animals is a criminal offence in the UK, as it is in many countries, and this extends to the practices in slaughterhouses. The government department that deals with such matters is Defra (the Department for the Environment, Food and Rural Affairs).

The Defra guidelines state that all killing or slaughter must be conducted without causing any avoidable excitement, pain or suffering to any animal. These strict guidelines state that all slaughter must be carried out by fully trained experts, all relevant licences must be held, only the permitted methods of slaughter can be used and every person involved in the process must be competent and acting with the animal's best interests at heart.

The two most common methods are by an overdose of barbiturates administered by a vet, or by the use of a captive bolt pistol. Both methods are very quick, but the noise of the pistol is very loud and therefore, if possible, the goat to be shot should be removed from the other animals.

The disposal of unwanted kids is also a problem that should be discussed with your vet. If, on the other hand, you are looking for a couple or a few rescue goats to start a new herd or add to one, go to page 91.

GENERAL
INFORMATION

HISTORY OF DOMESTICATED GOATS

Goats have been associated with man for centuries and are considered to be the oldest of domesticated farm animals. Beginning about 10,000—11,000 years ago, Neolithic farmers in the Near East began keeping small herds of goats for their milk and meat, and for their manure to be used for fuel, as well as for materials for clothing and building: hair, bone, skin and sinew.

Today there are more than 300 breeds of goats throughout the world, living in climates ranging from high altitude mountains to deserts. Recent research suggests that all goats today are descended from a handful of animals, and may have been domesticated in just a few different places. Archaeological data suggest two distinct places of domestication: the Euphrates river valley at Nevali Çori, Turkey and the Zagros Mountains of Iran at Ganj Dareh. Other possible sites of domestication include the Indus Basin in Pakistan at Mehrgarh and perhaps central Anatolia and the southern Levant. Other important archaeological areas with evidence for the initial process of goat domestication include Syria, Israel and Jordan (8500—7400 BC).

Domestication has been defined archaeologically by the presence and abundance of the animal into regions that were well beyond their normal habitats, by perceived changes in their body size and shape (called morphology) and by differences in demographic profiles in wild and domestic groups. Many people in industrialised nations, for whom cow's milk is often part of the standard diet, would not appreciate that the goat population of the world is significant and that, in fact, more people in the world drink milk from goats than from any other animal.

Goats are particularly populous in the continents of Asia and Africa, where their easy-going nature, low maintenance and size has seen them become a low-cost ally in the provision of meat and milk for a large portion of the population. It is estimated that over 80 per cent of the world's goat population is located in these two continents.

Dairy production from goats has become more of a commercialised operation in regions such as Europe, Oceania and North and South America, with cheese production being a significant industry in countries such as France.

The Food and Agriculture Organisation of the United Nations published a book *Observations on the Goat* in 1970, which provides many useful insights in to the history and benefits of goat milk. For example:

> *Archaeological evidence suggests that the goat is one of the oldest, if not the oldest, of the domesticated farm animals that has been associated with man for up to 10,000 years.*

> *In Greek mythology, the infant Zeus was*

reared on the milk-filled teats of the goat-nymph Amalthaea, whose image was commemoratively established among the stars of the Capricorn group.

In the literature at the beginning of the 20th century, it was not uncommon to see the goat recommended as a foster mother for children and books gave illustrations of children lying on a cushion to suckle the obliging nanny.

The goat played an important role in providing a vital part of the diet for early sailors and explorers. It is recorded that a goat accompanied Captain Cook on the *Endeavour* and wore a silver collar which said: 'The globe twice encircled, this the Goat, the second to the nurse of Jove, is thus rewarded for her never-failing milk.'

In addition, according to Chinese medicine, goat milk is believed to be of particular benefit to the throat and trachea. As described by Lee Su-Tan during the Ming dynasty, goat milk is a mild tonic food suitable for general good health.

The nutritional value of goat milk has been acknowledged by many cultures for centuries. However, the cow milk industry around the world has developed in a more sophisticated manner in terms of production, marketing and research compared with the goat milk industry. The key benefit that the cow milk industry enjoys is that cow milk can be produced more economically than goat milk, largely due to the greater productivity of the cow. However, the economic advantages do not necessarily mean that cow milk is more suitable for human consumption. In fact, many consider that goat milk is closer to human milk.

There has been less research into the nutritional benefits of goat milk compared with the millions spent on cow milk, but recently more investigation is being undertaken. This explains the advantages of goat milk and is providing a scientific basis to support the many centuries of anecdotal evidence.

GOAT PRODUCTS

DAIRY FOODS

Goat's milk is traditionally consumed fresh, fermented as yogurt or processed into butter and cheese. While goat's milk is a significant protein food in areas where grazing land is limited, goats lactate seasonally and produce lower quantities of milk than do cows, reducing availability. Fresh milk is a common beverage in South Asia, parts of the Middle East, and Greece and is an occasional dietary addition in other goat-raising nations (with the exception of China and Korea). In Europe, evaporated, canned, and powdered goat's milk products are popular. Cow's milk desserts are occasionally made from goat's milk as well, such as ice cream or the Latin American caramelised milk sweet known as dulce de leche or *cajeta*.

Goat's milk cheeses are favoured in the Middle East, and in parts of Europe and Latin America. They are processed and classified similarly to cheeses prepared from other milks. Soft and semisoft unripened (unaged) cheeses predominate, often homemade. Most are delicate, spreadable, snowy white in colour, with a light, tart flavour. Many are marketed under the generic term *Chèvre* (French for goat's cheese) and may be named for their shape, such as buttons or pyramids. Fewer firm and ripened (aged) goat's cheeses are produced; examples are Crottin and Sancerre. Some cheeses traditionally made with goat's, cow's, or sheep's milk blends include Feta, Fromage Frais, Gjetost, Kaseri, and Queso Fresco.

MEAT

Goat meat has a taste similar to mutton, with a slightly gamey flavour. It is lower in fat than either beef or mutton (due to a fat layer exterior to the muscle rather than marbled through it), and can be drier. The United States Department of Agriculture (USDA) describes quality goat meat as firm and finely grained. The colour can vary between females and males, from light pink to bright red. Kids, defined as under one year old, are often slaughtered at three to five months of age. Their meat is less flavourful and juicy, but more tender than the meat of older goats.

Goat meat is an important protein source in South Asia, the Middle East, and Africa. It is consumed regularly in some parts of Latin America, such as the Caribbean, Mexico, and Brazil, and is regionally popular in China, Korea, Indonesia, the Philippines, Greece, Italy, Portugal and Spain. The entire goat is usually consumed. An eviscerated carcass is typically cut, flesh and bone, into cubes for stewing, used in dishes such as curried goat and garlic-flavoured *caldereta*, a Spanish specialty found also in Latin America and the Philippines. Roasted goat is popular worldwide, often considered a special-occasion food. In Saudi Arabia, the cavity is stuffed with rice, fruits, and nuts. Jerked goat leg, heavily seasoned before cooking over allspice wood, is a Jamaican specialty. Organ meats are eaten, too. Goat's head soup is prepared in most regions where the meat is consumed. The dish is known as *isiewu* in Nigeria; the eyes are considered a delicacy. In Morocco, kidneys, liver, heart, lung, and pancreas are added to the meat to make goat tagine. In Kyrgyzstan, the testicles are roasted separately over the fire for consumption by men, and washed down with vodka. In the Philippines, *paklay* is an Ilocano specialty that combines goat intestines with sour fruits, such as unripe pineapple.

There are few taboos regarding goat meat, and it is accepted by all major religions that permit eating meat. Jewish consumption is often dependent on kosher processing, and for Muslims it must be slaughtered according to halal rules. In some regions goats, especially kids, are associated with certain religious holidays, particularly Passover, Easter, and Ramadan. When I lived in New York, if you were to walk in Italian neighbourhoods, you would always see kid hanging outside the Italian butchers at Easter time. Goat meat is usually classified as a hot or yang food in the Chinese philosophical system of yin/yang, and preferentially consumed during the winter months. Goat meat is not well-accepted by a majority of Americans due to the negative associations with goats eating rubbish and the unpleasant odour of the buck during rut. Exceptions are found among ethnic populations and in the Southwest, where Spanish-Mexican influences have popularised barbecued or pit-roasted *cabrito* (suckling kid). Enterprising goat ranchers in the United States market goat jerky and sausages as *cabrito*, or as the more French-sounding *chevon*.

HEALTH VALUE

Milk

Goat's milk is a vitamin- and mineral-rich protein food, shown to be a suitable substitute for cow's milk in feeding malnourished children. Yet, it is the differences in the fat, protein, and carbohydrate composition of goat's milk that account for its reputation as a healthy food. The fat contains a high proportion of small-and medium-chain fatty acids, which increases absorbability and contributes to the tangy flavour. It is lower in casein proteins than is cow's milk, resulting in much smaller curd (protein clump) formation in the stomach, another factor in digestibility. Goat's milk is naturally homogenized because it also lacks the protein agglutinin, so the fat stays dispersed in the milk and does not form cream at the top. Lactose, a sugar found in all milks, is slightly lower in goat's than in cow's milk, so individuals with lactose intolerance (the inability to digest lactose, resulting in intestinal discomfort) may tolerate goat's milk better.

Goat's milk is often touted as an alternative for individuals with allergies to cow's milk. Goat's milk may be better tolerated, yet it can cause adverse reactions in individuals who are extremely sensitive to caseins or other proteins, such as lactoglobulins. Some parents of infants and toddlers prefer goat's milk to cow's milk or baby formula due to its superior digestibility, but nutritional adequacy is dependent on fortification, particularly folate. And there is always the possibility that use of unpasteurised (raw) goat's milk or dairy foods can have serious health risks, including brucellosis (undulant fever), listeriosis, staphyloccus infection, salmonella poisoning and toxoplasmosis.

Meat

Goat meat is nutritionally notable for combining the advantages of red meat with those of white . meat or poultry. Goat meat provides similar amounts of protein when compared to the composite nutritional value for beef, but is 80 per cent lower in total fat, most of which is unsaturated. Goat meat is also lower in fat than pork, lamb, and skinless chicken breasts. Iron content in goat meat is 70 per cent higher than in beef and 200 per cent higher than chicken.

GENERAL INFORMATION ABOUT GOATS

Lifespan
10—14 years

Sexually mature
From 6 months

In season *(when female goat is fertile and can become pregnant)*
Between September and March; lasts up to 3 days. If not mated, females will come into season every 21 days. Once mated, goats can stay in milk for 2—3 years.

Gestation *(length of pregnancy)*
5 months

Number of offspring
1—4

Weaning *(coming off milk onto solid food)*
Not earlier than 10—12 weeks. The young need to eat increasing amounts of solid food from 2—3 weeks, in order to encourage rumen development and good condition.

Disbudding *(removing horn buds)*
3—7 days of age

Handling
Goats are sensitive, intelligent animals and should be handled in a smooth calm manner.

Companionship
Goats are social animals and are happier
in pairs. They do have a pecking order.

Health Problems
Diarrhoea (scouring) — seek advice from a
veterinary surgeon straight away.
Enterotoxemia — acute inflammation of the gut,
often fatal can be prevented by regular
vaccination.
Mastitis — inflamed swollen udder in females.
Caused by bacterial infection and encouraged by
bad hygiene. Seek a vet's advice.
Overgrown feet / foot rot — feet must be inspected
and trimmed every 4—6 weeks. Seek expert advice
on foot care.
Worms — symptoms include diarrhoea. Can be
prevented by regular worming. Seek a vet's advice
immediately.
Skin problems — A goat's skin ought to be clean and
well groomed. If there are any signs of
irritation or skin disease, seek a vet's advice.

FACTS AND
FANCIES

TWENTY TRUTHS ABOUT RAISING GOATS

By Suzanne Gasparotto

Mortality and goats go together. Any species that has early sexual maturity, short gestation and multiple births is going to have deaths — despite your efforts. Do your best and learn from your mistakes.

Confined goats become unhealthy or dead goats. Goats need many acres to roam in order to stay worm- and disease-free. You cannot successfully feedlot goats: they can't take the stress and crowding.

Unexpected problems will occur. Illnesses, weather problems, broken fences — when you raise goats, problems are going to occur at the most inconvenient time; when you are exhausted and when you can least afford it.

Trying to breed for all markets generally results in failure in most markets. Unless you have lots of acreage, cheap labour and a ton of money, you cannot produce quality breeding stock, show goats and slaughter animals. Each category is a specific type of animal and mutually exclusive of each other. Select one as your focal point and 'dabble' in the others — if you must.

If making the almighty pound is your driving force, you are doomed from the start. Focus on quality animals and honest business dealings and the money will follow.

Show goat and meat goats are not the same animal. If you want to raise meat goats, don't take nutrition or management advice from show goat people. Don't try to make show goats into breeding stock or commercial goats. Show goats are raised completely differently from meat goats.

Goats are not the 'tin can eating' animals of Saturday morning cartoon fame. Nutrition is the most complex part of raising goats. Rumens are very easy to upset. Think in terms of 'feeding the rumen, not the goat'. Have a qualified goat nutritionist review your specific needs and recommend a feeding programme adapted specifically to your herd. Improper feeding kills goats.

If someone offers you cheap bred does in the dead of winter, you can be sure that the deal is too good to be true. The act of moving them cross-country under such conditions is enough to make this a bad investment. The best you can expect is sick does and dead kids. Goats need time to adapt to new surroundings. Use common sense when transporting and relocating them.

Goats are livestock — not humans, dogs, or cats. They live outside, having a distinct social pecking order, and beat the heck out of each other regularly to maintain this ranking. Goats are delightful and intelligent animals, but they weren't created to live in the house with you. Lose the urbanite approach to raising goats.

A goat with a big rumen is not necessarily fat. A big rumen is indicative of a good digestive factory. A goat is a ruminant, and a ruminant is a pot-bellied animal. Fat on a goat layers around internal organs and also forms 'pones' or 'handles' that you can grab with your fingers at locations like where the chest meets the front leg. If you can pinch an inch of flesh at that point, the goat is likely fat. A light layer of subcutaneous fat over the ribs is essential.

Goats are NOT 'little cattle'. Goats and cattle are ruminants and there the similarity ends. Think of goats as 'first cousins' to deer in terms of how they live, roam and forage for food.

Goats are linear thinkers. The shortest distance between two points to a goat is a straight line. If you place a gate at the north end of the pasture and the home pens are south, goats are going to stand at the south end of the pasture until you have the sense to cut a gate there. If water is on the immediate other side of the fence, goats will not walk down and around the fence to get to the water. It's 'right over there,' so they'll stand in one place until you show them how to access the water or until they die of thirst. Cut a gate for

the water or until they die of thirst. Cut a gate for easy access and save yourself some grief. Learn to think like a goat.

A male goat has only one purpose in life — to reproduce his species in general and his lineage in particular. A buck in rut is a dangerous animal. He may have been cute when you were bottle feeding him, but he is a male on a mission when does are in heat — and you are in his way. Be careful around and always respect the danger potential of breeding bucks.

Bred does will kid in the worst possible weather. When sunshine changes to storms and the temperature drops below freezing, the kidding process will begin.

Bottle babies are a pain in the rear. Delightfully cute as they are, they grow up to be adults that are poorly socialised within the herd, overly-dependent upon humans and usually at the bottom of the herd's pecking order. Do everything you can — short of destroying a kid — to avoid bottle babies.

Goats are creatures of habit. If you have a goat that repeatedly hangs its horns in fencing, that goat will stick its head in the same place time after time until you fit the horns with a PVC pipe secured by duct tape. The grass is always greener on the other side of the fence.

Goats are HERD animals. More so than any other livestock, goats depend upon staying together for safety. They have few natural defences and many predators.

There is no such thing as a 'disease-free' herd. There isn't a goat alive that doesn't have something that could be deemed 'disease' in its system. The immune system requires a certain level of bacteria, worms, and coccidia in order to keep the goat healthy. No producer can guarantee totally 'disease-free' animals. When raising livestock, disease is a fact of life. You are never 'in control' to the extent that you want to be or think you are.

goat can get its head through the fence, the body is going to follow. Goats do not naturally have a 'reverse gear'. Fencing material designed especially for goats is a 'must'.

Cull or cope with your creation. Goats that are repeatedly sick, are overly susceptible to worms and coccidiosis, have chronic mastitis or foot rot/scald — such animals should be culled....

IMPORTANT! PLEASE READ THIS NOTICE!
All information provided in this article is based either on personal experience or information provided by others whose treatments and practices have been discussed fully with a vet for accuracy and effectiveness before passing them on to readers.
In all cases, it is your responsibility to obtain veterinary services and advice before using any of the information provided in this article.

Reprinted by permission from Suzanne Gasparotto, Onion Ranch Creek, Lohn, Texas.
www.tennesseemeatgoats.com
First published in *Goat Rancher* magazine

GOAT NEWS

Abstracted from an article in *The Times*,
Wednesday, November 5 2008.

Rob Crilly, Kogelo, Kenya

There's only one thing to take to a Kenyan election
victory feast: a goat. Preferably still breathing, a
sign of freshness and with big testicles, apparently
the sign of quality breeding.

And so it was that *The Times* bounced along a dirt
track towards the ancestral home of the Obamas in
a saloon car with the sound of John (inevitably its
name) bleating miserably from the boot. It had not
been easy finding such a quality specimen. The
local livestock market had mostly sheep and cattle,
with only a few scrawny goats on hand.

Instead, John was spotted at the side of the road by
my driver, George, who was impressed by the size
of its belly and other attributes. He was ours for
2500 shillings, a little under £20 and roughly the
price of 20 pints of beer or eight mosquito nets.

'This is a fine animal', said Abongo Malik Obama,
Barack's eldest half brother, at the lush family
homestead in the far west of Kenya. 'You are certainly
welcome now to stay and sit around the fire tonight'.

John was destined to become *nyama choma* — the
Swahili term for grilled meat — as one small part of
a vast celebration feast comprising four bulls, 16
chickens and assorted sheep and goats.

URBAN MYTHS

GOATS ARE GOOD LAWNMOWERS

Goats are not lawnmowers with legs. Although a goat's digestive system is similar to that of other ruminants, such as cattle and sheep, who are 'grazers' and eat grass, goats are more related to deer, who are 'browsers'. As browsers, goats are designed to eat, and prefer, brush and trees more than grass. Though goats will eat grass, if you are considering getting goats to be lawnmowers, you are going to be sorely disappointed, because they will eat your trees and roses before they will work on the lawn. Goats could be used to help reclaim grasslands that have been overgrown with brush. If you want to clear brushy land, a goat will be happy to help you with this project; if you want a lawnmower with legs, get a sheep, though a sheep probably will not be as loving and as smart as a goat will be.

SUDANESE MAN FORCED TO 'MARRY' GOAT

In February 2006, a BBC news story reported that a Sudanese man was forced to take a goat as his 'wife' after he was caught having sex with the animal.

Mr Alifi, of Hai Malakal in Upper Nile State, told the *Juba Post* newspaper that he heard a loud noise around midnight on 13 February and immediately rushed outside to find Mr Tombe with his goat.

'When I asked him: "what are you doing there?",
he fell off the back of the goat, so I captured and
tied him up.'

Mr Alifi then took him to a council of elders to
decide how to deal with the case.

'They said I should not take him to the police, but
rather let him pay a dowry for my goat because he
used it as his wife,' Mr Alifi told the newspaper
that Mr Tombe was ordered to pay a dowry of
15,000 Sudanese dinars (about £40) to him.

'We have given him the goat, and as far as we
know they are still together,' Mr Alifi said.

SUNDAY LUNCH

A young couple invited their elderly minister for
Sunday lunch. While they were in the kitchen
preparing the meal, the minister asked their son
what they were having to eat.
'Goat,' the little boy replied.
'Goat?' said the startled minister, 'are you sure
about that?'
'Yes,' said the youngster. 'I heard Dad say to Mum,
"today is as good as any day to have the old goat
for dinner".

GOAT JOKES

A rancher named Clyde had a car accident. In court, the trucking company's fancy lawyer was questioning Clyde. 'Didn't you say, at the scene of the accident, "I'm fine",' asked the lawyer.

Clyde responded, 'Well, I'll tell you what happened. I had just loaded my favourite goat, Bessie, into the...'

'I didn't ask for any details,' the lawyer interrupted. 'Just answer the question. Did you not say at the scene of the accident, "I'm fine!"?

Clyde said, 'Well, I had just got Bessie into the trailer and I was driving down the road...' The lawyer interrupted again and said, 'Judge, I am trying to establish the fact that, at the scene of the accident, this man told the Highway Patrolman on the scene that he was just fine. Now several weeks after the accident he is trying to sue my client. I believe he is a fraud. Please tell him to simply answer the question'.

By this time, the Judge was fairly interested in Clyde's answer and said to the lawyer, 'I'd like to hear what he has to say about his favourite goat, Bessie'.

Clyde thanked the Judge and proceeded, 'Well as I was saying, I had just loaded Bessie, my favourite goat, into the trailer and was driving her down the highway when this huge semi-truck and trailer ran the stop sign and smacked my truck right in the side. I was thrown into one ditch and Bessie was thrown into the other. I was hurting real bad and didn't want to move. However, I could hear old Bessie moaning and groaning. I knew she was in terrible shape just by her groans. Shortly after the accident a highway patrolman came on the scene. He could hear Bessie moaning and groaning so he went over to her. After he looked at her, he took out his gun and shot her between the eyes. Then the patrolman came across the road, gun in hand, looked at me, and said, "How are you feeling?"

'Now what the hell would you say?'

• • • • •

One night a burglar is trying to break into a house. Crossing the lawn he hears a voice — 'Jesus is watching you'. He turns around but doesn't see anything. So he starts crossing the lawn again. 'Jesus is watching you' he hears again.

Looking around he sees a goat on a chain by the side of the house.

He says to the goat, 'Did you say that?'
The goat replies, 'Yes I did.'
'What's your name?' he asks.
'Clarence.'
The burglar says, 'What kind of stupid idiot would name his goat Clarence?'
The goat laughs and says, 'The same stupid idiot who named his Rottweiler Jesus.'

RECIPES

YOGURT AND SIMPLE CHEESE MAKING

Yogurt made from goat's milk has been eaten for centuries throughout the Balkans, the Middle East and India, where goats are the standard dairy animals. Homemade yogurt is so superior to yogurt bought from shops that no comparison is possible.

There are several ways of making it, but the beginning steps are all the same. To make the first batch (1.2 kg/about 2½ lb).

You will need:
    1 litre goat's milk
    5 tablespoons dried milk powder (preferably
       goat's milk)
    200 g (7 oz) organic goat's yogurt (this will
       be your starter)

You will also need:
    a milk pan
    a jug
    a sieve
    a spoon
    sterilised glass jars to store the yogurt

1. First, stir the dried milk into the liquid milk and heat together in the milk pan until it is almost boiling (there will be small bubbles around the side of the pan).
2. Remove the pan from the heat and allow to cool to body temperature (37°C/98.6°F).
3. When the milk is cool, pour it into the jug

through the sieve. Add the starter yogurt. This can either be store bought or from a previous batch of homemade yogurt.

You can either pour the mixture into a preheated thermos flask, wrapped in towels to retain the heat, or put it into a casserole in a warm oven and leave overnight with the oven turned off, or 'cook' it in a yogurt maker. I have an electric yogurt maker with little glass pots that you can store in the refrigerator. All of these methods should produce superb yogurt in about 5—6 hours. When the yogurt is done, store in suitable containers in the refrigerator.

YOGURT SOFT CHEESE

Makes about 1 kg (2¼ lb)

Pour the yogurt into a muslin-lined colander and put in the kitchen sink. Leave it to set all day or overnight, until the whey drains off and the yogurt becomes a light, creamy cheese. Use at once in place of cream cheese, or refrigerate in a covered container for up to one week.

You can form the cheese into small balls, roll them in olive oil and sprinkle them with paprika or herbs.

You can also make a delicious dessert tart by combining about 675 g (1½ lb) of newly-made yogurt cheese with 45 ml (3 tablespoons) honey and 5 ml (1 teaspoon) vanilla essence or grated orange rind. Stir until smooth and pour into a baked tart shell. Chill in the refrigerator for 24 hours before serving, either as is, or topped with fresh fruit in season.

BASIC CURD CHEESE

This cheese can be made in a mould to give it a definite shape or in a bag or cloth.

To every 4½ litres of milk at 25°C (77°F), add 3.5 ml (¾ teaspoon) starter and stir thoroughly. Then add 1 ml (¼ teaspoon) animal rennet or 0.5 ml (⅛ teaspoon) vegetarian rennet. The rennet must be diluted with six times its volume of cold water and stirred into the milk. Top stir the milk until coagulation begins (you will feel the milk begin to thicken–do not overstir) and then leave for 3–5 hours by which time a firm curd should have formed. Using a slotted spoon, ladle the curd in thin, even slices into a mould standing on a mat and board or into a cloth hung over a colander. Leave to drain for 12–24 hours. Remove the mould when the cheese is firm enough to stand without losing shape, then turn onto a clean mat and stand for a further 12 hours before lightly salting on the sides and packing.

This cheese will keep in a refrigerator for up to seven days. If you have made your cheese in a cloth, the salt can be mixed into the curd after scraping it into a bowl and before packing it into pots.

The smoothness of the cheese is determined almost entirely by the time taken to set the milk. The longer the time, the smoother and creamier the cheese. A good average time is about five hours. If it takes any longer than this, the curd is difficult to drain; if it takes only an hour or so, the cheese will be tough. The time taken for the milk to set is determined by three things:

- The freshness of the milk. It is recommended that the milk should be 12 hours old.

- The temperature of the milk during setting. At body temperature (37°C/98.6°F), the setting is very rapid, while at 16°C/60.8°F it is very slow. It is usual to add rennet between 21 and 27°C (70–80°F).

- The quantity and quality of the rennet used. To test the strength of the rennet, milk a measured 150 ml (5 fl oz) straight into a warm bottle and add 3 drops of rennet, mixing quickly. It should take four minutes to set. If it takes longer, the rennet is weaker and the amount needed should be determined.

Basic curd cheese recipe from *Easy Dairying*, published by the British Goat Society. If you want to get into serious fancy cheese making, you really should get this or another cheese making book.

STARTERS AND SOUPS

CHEESE SOUFFLÉ

You will need   Serves 4

    30 ml (2 tablespoons) grated Parmesan cheese

    30 ml (2 tablespoons) unsalted butter

    60 ml (4 tablespoons) flour

    120 ml (4 fl oz) fresh goat's milk

    30 ml (2 tablespoons) dry white wine

    5 ml (1 teaspoon) Dijon mustard

    100 g (3½ oz) fresh goat's cheese, crumbled

    7.5 ml (1½ teaspoons) fresh thyme leaves *or*

      2.5 ml (½ teaspoon dried thyme)

    salt and freshly ground black pepper

    2 large eggs, separated, plus 3 large egg whites

    60 ml (4 tablespoons) sharp Cheddar cheese

1. Preheat the oven to 190°C (375°F/Gas Mark 5).
Butter a 1-litre soufflé dish. Add the Parmesan and
rotate the dish to coat it with the cheese.
2. In a medium saucepan, melt the butter over a
low heat. Add the flour and cook, whisking, until
blended. Whisk in the milk, wine and mustard and
cook, whisking, until the sauce is smooth and thick,
about 8 minutes. Remove from the heat and stir in
the goat's cheese and 1 teaspoon of the thyme
leaves. Season with salt and pepper and stir in the
egg yolks. Scrape the soufflé mixture into a large
bowl and press a piece of clingfilm directly on the
surface.
3. In a large bowl, beat the egg whites with a
pinch of salt until soft peaks form. Using a rubber
spatula, fold one-third of the beaten whites into

the soufflé mixture; fold in the remaining whites
until just a few streaks remain.
4. Gently scrape the mixture into the prepared
dish. Sprinkle the top with the Cheddar, the
remaining 1/2 teaspoon of thyme and some pepper.
Bake the soufflé in the centre of the oven for
about 25 minutes, or until nicely risen and browned
on top. Serve at once.

COCKTAIL CHEESE BALLS

You will need **Makes 50—60**

    115 g (4 oz) pecan pieces

    15 g (1/2 oz) unsalted butter, melted

    2.5 ml (1/2 teaspoon) brown sugar

    2.5 ml (1/2 teaspoon) salt

    340 g (12 oz) soft goat's cheese

    5 ml (1 teaspoon) finely chopped rosemary

    5 ml (1 teaspoon) coriander seeds, crushed in pestle
      and mortar

    2.5 ml (1/2 teaspoon) freshly ground black pepper

    About 50—60 flat-leaf parsley leaves

1. Preheat the oven to 200°C (400°F/Gas Mark 6)
and place rack in the upper third.
2. Toss pecans with butter, sugar and salt, then
toast in a baking tray until fragrant and a shade
darker, 8—10 minutes. Transfer to a plate and cool
completely.
3. Pulse pecans in a food processor just until finely
chopped, then transfer to a wide shallow bowl.
4. Stir together goat's cheese, rosemary, coriander,
and pepper until well-combined. Form teaspoonsful
of the cheese mixture into balls between your

palms, then coat with pecans. Transfer to a serving plate.

5. Press a parsley leaf on top of each ball and spear with a wooden toothpick.

Put a parsley leaf under each cheese ball and spear together with a wooden pick.

Adapted from a recipe in *Gourmet* Magazine.

GOAT'S CHEESE AND ASPARAGUS PIZZA

You will need   Serves 4–6

For the pizza base:
>   5 g (1 teaspoon) active dry yeast
>   60 ml (4 tablespoons) tepid water
>   240 ml (8 fl oz) cold water
>   5 ml (1 teaspoon) salt
>   approximately 450 g (1 lb) bread flour
>   Olive oil

1. Sprinkle the yeast over the warm water in a large bowl. Let stand to froth for 5-10 minutes. Stir in the cold water and salt, then add the flour, about one-fourth at a time. When enough flour has been added, the dough can be removed from the bowl to a floured work surface.

2. Knead until smooth, about 10 minutes and form into a ball. Pour a little olive oil into the bowl and roll the dough around to coat. Cover the bowl with a tea cloth and set aside to rise for about 1½–2 hours.

3. After the dough has risen, remove from the bowl to a floured work surface and punch it down. If

using immediately, roll out to a circle approximately 30 cm (12 inches) and prepare the topping. If you are going to be baking it later, refrigerate the ball of dough, taking it out of the fridge about an hour before needed.

For the topping:
    400 g (14 oz) tin chopped tomatoes, drained
    12 asparagus spears, trimmed, cut in half lengthwise
      if thick and then cut into 4-cm (1½-inch) pieces
    45 ml (3 tablespoons) extra-virgin olive oil
    170 g (6 oz) fresh goat's cheese, crumbled
    15 ml (1 tbsp) dried Italian herbs or dried oregano
    1.25 ml (¼ teaspoon) dried crushed chilli peppers

1. Preheat the oven to 200°C (400°F/Gas Mark 4).
2. Put the rolled out pizza base on a pizza tin or baking tray. Spread the base with the tomatoes. Top with the asparagus and drizzle with olive oil. Bake for 5 minutes.
3. Crumble the goat's cheese over the pizza and sprinkle with herbs and dried chillies. Bake until the edges of the dough are golden, about 9 minutes further.
4. Cut into wedges and serve, either as a starter, or as a light lunch or supper.

GOAT'S CHEESE CAKES WITH
TOMATO—OLIVE SALAD

You will need   **Serves 4**

    200 g (7 oz) fresh goat's cheese

    10 ml (2 teaspoons) chopped thyme

    salt and freshly ground black pepper

    60 ml (4 tablespoons) breadcrumbs

    45 ml (3 tablespoons) flour

    2 large egg yolks, beaten

    olive oil to sprinkle

For the tomato and olive salad:

    1 clove garlic, finely chopped

    15 ml (1 tablespoon) balsamic vinegar

    45 ml (3 tablespoons) extra-virgin olive oil

    250 g (9 oz) cherry or plum tomatoes, halved if large

    30 g (1 oz) pitted Greek olives

    basil or thyme leaves to garnish

1. Mix the goat's cheese, thyme and seasoning in a bowl. Divide into eight and shape each into a cake. Refrigerate for several hours to firm up.
2. Preheat the oven to 200°C (400°F/Gas Mark 6).
3. Spread the breadcrumbs on a sheet of parchment paper. Remove the cheese from the fridge. Put the flour and egg yolks in separate dishes. Dip each cheese cake in flour, then in egg and then in breadcrumbs.
4. Place on a parchment covered baking tray, sprinkle with a little olive oil and bake for 5—10 minutes on each side, until golden. Remove from the oven.

5. Make the salad. Add the garlic, vinegar and olive oil to a screw top jar and shake until combined.

6. To serve, portion the tomatoes and olives, pour a little dressing over and set two cheese cakes on each plate. Garnish with basil or thyme leaves.

GOAT'S CHEESE WITH OLIVES, LEMON AND THYME

Whenever you need a quick but impressive starter, or something different to serve with drinks, this is sure to please. Warming the olives in a thyme and lemon rind infused oil really wakes up the flavour and transforms a goat's cheese log into a wonderful topping for toasted ciabatta.

You will need   **Serves 4**

    115 g (4 oz) assorted olives

    3 fresh thyme sprigs

    45 ml (3 tablespoons) extra-virgin olive oil

    2.5 ml ($\frac{1}{2}$ teaspoon) grated lemon rind

    1.25 ml ($\frac{1}{4}$ teaspoon) freshly ground black pepper

    125 g ($4\frac{1}{2}$ oz) goat's cheese log, cut into 4 slices

    4 slices ciabatta bread

1. Heat the olives, thyme, olive oil, lemon rind and pepper in a small saucepan over a low heat until fragrant (do not simmer). Cool to room temperature.

2. Toast the ciabatta. Cover with a slice of goat's cheese and a spoonful of the olive mixture.

LEEK AND POTATO SOUP

You will need   Serves 4

    800 g (1 lb 12 oz) leeks, trimmed

    30 g (1 oz) butter

    450 g (1 lb) potatoes, peeled and diced

    600 ml (1 pint) fresh goat's milk

    600 ml (1 pint) vegetable stock

    salt and freshly ground white pepper

    Crusty bread and flavoured butter to serve*

1. Wash the leeks well, dry and roughly chop.
2. Melt the butter in a large saucepan and add the leeks. Cook until slightly softened, then add the diced potatoes, milk and vegetable stock. Bring to the simmer and simmer gently until the potatoes are cooked and the leeks are soft. Remove from the heat.
3. Pour the contents of the saucepan into a blender or food processor and liquidise, adding salt and pepper to taste. Alternatively, leave the soup in the saucepan and liquidise with a stick blender if you have one.
4. Reheat and serve hot with crusty bread, spread with flavoured butter.

*Flavoured butter is so easy to make. Just add herbs such as basil, parsley or rosemary to softened butter, add grated lemon or lime rind and form into a disc or log. You can also add spices to softened butter, like paprika, cumin, or whatever you fancy.

SAVOURY GOAT'S CHEESECAKE WITH PESTO

'Cheesecake' usually evokes taste memories of thick and creamy slabs of sweetness. Here's a savoury appetiser version to spread on toasted baguette slices and enjoy with pre-dinner drinks. Whenever I serve this, I spread a few toasts with the cheesecake and place them on the serving plate to avoid confusion on how to serve.

You will need   **Makes 12 servings**

For the cheesecake:

15 ml (1 tablespoon) unsalted butter, softened

22 ml (1½ tablespoons) dried breadcrumbs

340 g (12 oz) rindless goat's cheese (chevre), such as Bucheron or Montrachet, at room temperature

2 large eggs, at room temperature

340 g (12 oz) cream cheese, at room temperature

115 g (4 oz) soured cream

15 ml (1 tablespoon) cornflour

1.25 ml (¼ teaspoon) freshly ground black pepper

250 g (9 oz) pesto, homemade or store bought

For the toasts:

1 baguette loaf French or Italian bread, sliced 5 mm (¼-inch) thick

60 ml (4 tablespoons) extra-virgin olive oil

1. First make the cheesecake: preheat the oven to 150ºC (300°F/Gas Mark 2).
2. Using kitchen paper, coat the inside of a 20 cm (8-inch) springform tin with the butter. Sprinkle with the breadcrumbs and turn to coat with the

with the breadcrumbs and turn to coat with the butter. Pat the crumbs down in the tin and wrap the outside of the tin tightly with aluminium foil.

3. In a large bowl, using a hand-held electric mixer at medium speed, whisk the goat's cheese and eggs until smooth. Gradually whisk in the cream cheese, beating until smooth again. Whisk in the soured cream, cornflour and pepper. Spread evenly in the prepared tin. Place the tin in a large baking tray and add enough hot water to come 2.5 cm (1 inch) up the sides.

4. Bake until the cheesecake is puffed and very lightly browned around the edges, about 1 hour. Remove from the water bath. Run a sharp knife around the edges of the tin to release the cake. Cool completely on a wire rack. Remove the sides of the tin and wrap the cake in clingfilm. Chill at least 4 hours or overnight. (The cheesecake can be prepared up to 2 days ahead, covered and refrigerated.)

5. To make the toasts: increase the oven temperature to 200°C (400°F/Gas Mark 6). Place the baguette slices on baking sheets and brush with olive oil. Bake until lightly browned and crisp, about 10 minutes. Cool completely. (The toasts can be prepared up to 8 hours ahead, stored in plastic bags at room temperature.)

6. When ready to serve, transfer the cheesecake to a serving plate. Spread the top with pesto, allowing excess pesto to run down the sides. Arrange the toasts around the cheesecake. Let stand at room temperature for about 1 hour before serving. Spread a bit of pesto-topped cheesecake on a few toasts and place around the cheesecake. Allow guests to serve themselves.

ROASTED BEETROOT WITH GOAT'S CHEESE AND BALSAMIC VINEGAR

You will need   Serves 6

600 g (1 lb 5oz) fresh raw beetroot

3 small red onions, quartered

4 cloves garlic

45 ml (3 tablespoons) balsamic vinegar

60 ml (4 tablespoons) olive oil

salt and freshly ground black pepper

1 fresh rosemary sprig

115 g (4 oz) fresh goat's cheese, crumbled

30 ml (2 tablespoons) chopped flat leaf parsley

1. Preheat the oven to 190°C (375°F/Gas Mark 5).
2. Wash the beetroot in cold water and trim the stalks and roots. Cut larger beetroot in quarters and small ones in half.
3. Line a medium roasting tin with a double layer of aluminium foil, long enough to cover and seal the vegetables. Place the beetroot, onions and garlic on the foil, drizzle over the balsamic vinegar and olive oil, season with salt and pepper and tuck in the rosemary sprig. Seal the foil tightly around the vegetables.
4. Bake in the centre of the oven for 1½ hours.
5. Open up the foil and continue to cook for a further 40 minutes or until the beetroot is tender.
6. Remove from the oven and allow to cool. Slice the beetroot thickly, arrange in a serving dish and pour over any pan juices.
7. Scatter the crumbled goat's cheese over and sprinkle with parsley.

MAIN DISHES

CARDAMOM GOAT (*ELAICHI GOSHT*)

You will need   **Serves 4—6**

30 green cardamoms

15 ml (1 tablespoon) olive oil

15 ml (1 tablespoon) coarsely ground black pepper

1 kg (2.2 lb) boneless goat meat in bite-sized cubes

15 ml (1 tablespoon) turmeric

15 ml (1 tablespoon) ground coriander

5 ml (1 teaspoon) chilli powder

100 g (3½ oz) goat's yogurt

4 tomatoes, skinned and finely chopped

salt to taste

480 ml (16 fl oz) hot water

coriander sprigs, chopped

naan bread to serve

1. Grind cardamoms to a powder with a pestle and mortar. Add 15 ml (1 tablespoon) water and make a paste.
2. Heat oil in a large saucepan or wok. Add the cardamom paste and pepper and sauté over a low heat for 2—3 minutes.
3. Add the meat and turn well, ensuring that the meat is well-coated with the cardamom and pepper. Add the turmeric, ground coriander and chilli powder. Mix well and sauté the meat in the spices for a full 10 minutes over a low heat. Turn constantly to ensure the spices don't burn and the meat doesn't stick to the pan.
4. Add the yogurt, tomatoes and salt to taste. Sauté for another 5 minutes.

5. Add the water, bring to the boil and reduce the heat. Cover the saucepan and cook until the meat is tender, 45—60 minutes.

6. Garnish with the chopped coriander and serve with naan bread.

GOAT-STUFFED CHICKEN

You will need   **Serves 6**

    2.5 kg (5½ lb) whole chicken, boned*

Stuffing:

    1 kg (2.2 lb) minced goat meat

    1 clove garlic, crushed

    chopped fresh coriander, marjoram, basil and thyme

    15 ml (1 tablespoon) dry white wine

    30 ml (2 tablespoons) tomato purée

    splash of Worcestershire sauce

    ½ onion, finely chopped

    2 eggs, beaten

    1 large slice of white bread

    olive oil

1. Put the goat meat in a large mixing bowl and add to it the garlic, herbs, wine, tomato purée, Worcestershire sauce and onion.

2. Mix together thoroughly with a wooden spoon or your hands. Add eggs and mix again. Tear the bread into small pieces, add to the goat mixture and mix until the stuffing becomes firm.

3. Lay the chicken, skin-side down on a board, stuff with the goat mixture and sew closed.

4. Preheat the oven to 180°C (350°F/Gas Mark 4).

5. Put the chicken in a roasting tin, stitched side

until the stuffing becomes firm.

3. Lay the chicken, skin-side down on a board, stuff with the goat mixture and sew closed.
4. Preheat the oven to 180°C (350°F/Gas Mark 4).
5. Put the chicken in a roasting tin, stitched side down, cover with aluminium foil and roast for 1 hour.
6. Brush the chicken with olive oil and turn up the heat to 200°C (400°F/Gas Mark 6). Check for doneness after 30 minutes. Keep checking until chicken is almost done (an oven thermometer inserted into the chicken makes this easier).
7. When the chicken is almost cooked, remove the foil and let the chicken brown for about 15 minutes. Allow about 2 hours in all.
8. Serve sliced with roast potatoes and vegetables.

*Any good basic cookery book will show you how to bone a chicken. Alternatively, if you are purchasing your chicken, ask your butcher to do it for you.

KID KEBABS

You will need   Serves 4–6

  1 kg (2.2 lb) boneless goat meat cut into 2.5 cm
    (1-inch) cubes
  60 ml (4 tablespoons) olive oil
  Juice of half a lemon
  2 cloves garlic
  15 ml (1 tablespoon) soy sauce
  15 ml (1 tablespoon) sherry
  2 bay leaves
  rosemary sprigs, chopped

1. Marinate the goat meat cubes in a mixture of the oil, lemon, crushed garlic, soy sauce, sherry, bay leaves, marjoram and pepper. Leave for at least two hours or overnight.
2. Drain the marinade into a bowl and set aside.
3. Preheat the grill to high.
4. Thread the meat pieces onto the skewers alternatively with the onions, sweetcorn, mushrooms and peppers (2 or 3 pieces of pepper together will reduce overcooking).
5. Grill the kebabs for 10–15 minutes or until the meat is tender, turning and basting with the marinade often.
6. Serve with rosemary and herb potato wedges and salad.

MEXICAN GOAT STEW (*BIRRIA DE JALISCO*)

You will need   **Serves 10**

Adobo sauce:
  8 dried ancho chillies
  ½ onion
  2 cloves garlic
  5 ml (1 teaspoon) oregano
  salt to taste
  60 ml (2 fl oz) vinegar

  9 kg (20 lb) goat meat on the bone, cut into chunks
  Salt and freshly ground pepper to taste

Tomato salsa:
  6 red tomatoes
  6 green tomatoes
  ½ onion

2 cloves garlic

5 ml (1 teaspoon) oregano

2 whole cloves

6 black peppercorns

5 ml (1 teaspoon) sesame seeds

2.5 ml (½ teaspoon) ground ginger

1 cm (½ inch) cinnamon stick

30 ml (2 tablespoons) grated plain chocolate

salt to taste

1.4 litres (2.4 pints) water

Lime juice, chopped coriander, chopped raw onion and tortillas to serve

1. Place chillies, onion, garlic, oregano and salt in a small saucepan. Cover with water and boil until onions are soft.

2. Place in blender and mix well.

3. Add the vinegar.

4. Season the goat meat and place in an ovenproof casserole.

5. Pour the adobo sauce over the meat, cover with a tight-fitting lid and bake in a 180°C (350°F/Gas Mark 4) oven for at least 4 hours, until the meat falls off the bone.

6. Meanwhile, place all the salsa ingredients in a medium saucepan and cook until the onion is soft. Remove from the heat and purée the sauce in a blender. After the meat is cooked, take some of the stock and add it to the salsa for additional flavour.

7. To serve, pour tomato salsa over the meat in the adobo sauce. Serve with lime juice, chopped coriander and chopped raw onion sprinkled on top and accompany with tortillas to soak up the juices.

WEST INDIAN GOAT CURRY

You will need   **Serves 6–8**

 2.3 kg (5 lb) goat meat from leg, with or without bone

 30 ml (2 tablespoons) rapeseed oil

 1 clove garlic, finely chopped

 60 ml (4 tablespoons) curry powder

 5 ml (1 teaspoon) ground coriander

 10 ml (2 teaspoons) turmeric

 5 ml (1 teaspoon) ground cumin

 2.5 ml ($\frac{1}{2}$ teaspoon) dried thyme or 1 sprig fresh thyme

 2.5 ml ($\frac{1}{2}$ teaspoon) ground ginger

 freshly ground black pepper to taste

 1 small Scotch bonnet chilli, finely chopped

 1 large carrot, sliced

 1 large onion, chopped

 400 g (14 oz) tinned tomatoes

 480 ml (16 fl oz) chicken stock

 60 ml (4 tablespoons) dark soy sauce

 1 kg (2.2 lb) potatoes, peeled and cut into 2.5 cm
   (1 inch) cubes

 Cooked white rice and fried ripe plantains or cooked,
 cubed pumpkin to serve

1. Brown the meat in the oil on all sides in a flameproof casserole, then remove and set aside.
2. Add all the spices to the oil and allow them to blend together without browning.
3. Add the carrot, onion and tomatoes to the spices and cook together for a few minutes.
4. Add the browned meat, mixing it well with the ingredients in the casserole.
5. Add the chicken stock. Cook on a medium-low heat for 40 minutes.

6. Add the soy sauce and potatoes. Cook for a further 30 minutes, stirring occasionally until the potatoes are cooked.

7. Serve on a bed of white rice, accompanied by fried ripe plantains or pumpkin.

Recipe supplied by my sister, Susan de Robles, who usually cooks this for a dozen or more people at her home in St Maarten, Netherlands Antilles.

ROAST GOAT

You will need   **Serves 4**

    1 goat leg joint
    fresh rosemary
    streaky bacon

1. Preheat the oven to 180°C (350°F/Gas Mark 4). Weigh the leg joint.

2. Using a sharp knife make approximately 12 small cuts into the thickest parts of the meat.

3. Push a piece of bacon and a sprig of rosemary into each of the slits.

4. Pour the water and salt (mixed together) into a roasting tin and lay in the joint of meat.

5. Place small pieces of the butter randomly over the top surface of the joint.

6. Roast for 20 minutes per pound. Check for doneness with an instant read meat thermometer.

7. Remove from the oven, leave to rest for 15 minutes or so and then carve into slices.

8. Serve with seasonal vegetables and roast potatoes.

From www.goat-meat.co.uk

BREADS

CHILLI CORNBREAD

Serves 4—8, depending on greediness

This would be excellent served with stews and casseroles. In the American southwest, cornbread often accompanies chilli.

You will need
  280 g (10 oz) fine maize meal or polenta
  85 g (3 oz) plain flour
  10 ml (2 teaspoons) bicarbonate of soda
  salt and freshly ground black pepper
  1 large egg
  150 ml (5 fl oz) fresh goat's milk
  425 g (15 oz) fresh goat's yogurt
  2 large red chillies, seed and finely chopped

1. Preheat the oven to 190°C (375°F/Gas Mark 5). Butter a 20 cm (8-inch) square or similar baking tin.
2. Combine the maize meal or polenta, flour and bicarbonate of soda in a large bowl. Season to taste. In a jug, combine the egg, goat's milk, yogurt and chillies.
3. Make a well in the dry ingredients and pour in the contents of the jug into the well. Stir lightly to combine. Do not over-mix or the bread will be tough.
4. Pour the batter into the baking tin and bake for 35—40 minutes until a toothpick inserted into the centre of the bread comes away clean and the bread is firm and golden on top. Remove from the

oven.

5. Serve warm, cut into squares.

N.B. This bread can be wrapped in aluminium foil and frozen for up to 1 month.

GOAT'S CHEESE AND CHIVES SCONES

You will need   **Makes 8 large scones**

225 g (8 oz) plain flour

10 ml (2 teaspoons) baking powder

5 ml (1 teaspoon) sugar

2.5 ml (1/2 teaspoon) bicarbonate of soda

2.5 ml (1/2 teaspoon) salt

1.25 ml (1/4 teaspoon) freshly ground black pepper

55 g (2 oz) chilled butter, cut into 1-cm (1/2-inch) cubes

handful of fresh chives, chopped

140 g (5 oz) fresh goat's cheese, crumbled

225 g (8 fl oz) goat's yogurt or 240 ml (8 fl oz) goat's
    buttermilk

a little goat's milk to brush

1. Preheat the oven to 200°C (400°F/Gas Mark 6). Line a heavy baking sheet with parchment paper.
2. Whisk flour, baking powder, sugar, bicarbonate of soda, salt and pepper in a large bowl. Using fingertips, rub butter into dry ingredients until coarse meal forms. Stir in the chives. Add cheese and yogurt or buttermilk; stir with a fork just until a sticky dough forms (bits of cheese will be visible in dough).
3. Turn dough out onto a lightly floured surface and knead gently 8 times with floured hands. Do not over-knead! Form into a round, about 2 to 2.5

cm (³⁄₄-inch to 1 inch) thick. Cut the round into 8 wedges. Use a pastry brush to brush goat's milk over the surface of the wedges.

4. Arrange wedges about 1 cm (¹⁄₂ inch) apart on the prepared baking sheet and bake in the centre of the oven until golden brown, about 20 minutes. Cool slightly on a rack. These are best eaten just baked and warm, with a little butter.

RED PEPPER CHEESE BREAD

This is delicious served with soups and stews on a cold evening.

You will need   **Serves 6-8**

    225 g (8 oz) wholemeal flour

    225 g (8 oz) plain flour, plus extra for dusting

    5 ml (1 teaspoon) bicarbonate of soda

    10 ml (2 teaspoons) baking powder

    5 ml (1 teaspoon) salt

    5 ml (1 teaspoon) caster sugar

    30 g (1 oz) butter, melted

    300 ml (10 fl oz) goat's milk at room temperature

    170 g (6 oz) hard goat's cheese, grated

    45 ml (3 tablespoons) pumpkin seeds

    85 g (3 oz) roasted peppers from a jar, drained
      and chopped

1. Preheat the oven to 190°C (375°F/Gas Mark 5).
2. Sift the flour, bicarbonate of soda, baking powder, salt and sugar into a large bowl and make a well in the centre. Combine the butter and milk and pour into the well. Mix to a soft dough. Add most of the cheese, 30 ml (2 tablespoons) of the

pumpkin seeds and the chopped peppers to the dough.

3. Dust the work surface with flour. Turn the dough out of the bowl onto the floured surface and knead to combine. Divide the dough in eighths and form into rounds about 4 cm (1½ inches) high. Place the rounds side by side on a floured baking sheet, scatter the remaining cheese and pumpkin seeds on top and bake for 30 minutes until golden brown.

4. Remove from the oven, cool on a wire rack and serve warm.

DESSERTS

BAKED VANILLA CHEESECAKES WITH RASPBERRY SAUCE

You will need   **Serves 8**

For the crust:

55 g (2 oz) butter, plus extra for greasing

170 g (6 oz) chocolate biscuits, crushed into crumbs

55 g (2 oz) pecan nuts, finely chopped

15 g (1 tablespoon) caster sugar

For the filling:

280 g (10 oz) full-fat soft cheese

170 g (6 oz) fresh goat's cheese

250 g (9 oz) mascarpone cheese

55 g (2 oz) caster sugar

5 ml (1 teaspoon) vanilla essence

4 eggs, beaten

For the sauce:

55 g (2 oz) caster sugar

250 g (9 oz) fresh raspberries, plus fresh raspberries
to serve

1. Preheat the oven to 180°C (350°F/Gas Mark 4).
Grease 8 ramekins with butter.
2. Melt the 55 g/2 oz butter in a saucepan, then
mix in the chocolate biscuit crumbs, pecans and
sugar. Divide this mixture equally amongst the
ramekins, pressing firmly into the base. Bake for
10 minutes, then remove from the oven and reduce
the oven temperature to 150°C (300°F/Gas Mark 2).

3. Whisk together the three cheeses, sugar, vanilla essence and eggs until smooth.

4. Place the prepared ramekins on a baking tray and pour the filling evenly into them. Bake for 30 minutes until just set. Remove from the oven and set aside to cool.

5. Cover the ramekins with clingfilm and refrigerate for up to two days.

6. Make the sauce. Heat the sugar with 60 ml (2 fl oz) water until syrupy, about 5 minutes. Stir in the raspberries and cook for about 2 minutes. Remove from the heat. (You can remove the raspberry pips by sieving them, but I wouldn't bother because I like that bit of texture.)

7. To serve, remove the ramekins from the fridge and run a thin knife around the edges. Unmould onto serving plates, drizzle with raspberry sauce and scatter a few fresh raspberries around.

CHEESECAKE WITH ROASTED HERBED PEARS

This cheesecake is a delicious finale for a sophisticated dinner party.

You will need   Serves 12

For the crust:

    170 g (6 oz) digestive biscuits

    55 g (2 oz) sliced almonds

    30 g (2 tablespoons) caster sugar

    55 g (2 oz) unsalted butter, melted

Filling:

    450 g (1 lb) cream cheese, cut into pieces

    340 g (12 oz) fresh goat's cheese, crumbled

    10 ml (2 teaspoons) grated lemon rind

    30 ml (2 tablespoons) fresh lemon juice

    5 ml (1 teaspoon) vanilla essence

    280 g (10 oz) caster sugar

    4 eggs, beaten

Herbed pears:

    6 ripe, firm Comice or Williams pears

    15ml (1 tablespoon) unsalted butter

    15 ml (1 tablespoon) fresh lemon juice

    60 ml (4 tablespoons) maple syrup

    240 ml (8 fl oz) apple and pear juice,divided

    2 sprigs fresh rosemary, crushed

    10 ml (2 teaspoons) cornflour, mixed with 15 ml
       (1 tablespoon) water

1. Preheat the oven to 200°C (400°F/Gas Mark 6).
2. Process the digestive biscuits in a food processor until they are almost ground to a powder. Add the almonds and sugar and continue to process until almonds are ground.
3. Transfer the crumb mixture to a bowl and add the butter. Stir until combined. Press the crumb mixture into the base of a 23-cm (9-inch) spring-form cake tin.
4. Place the tin on a baking tray and bake until the crust is golden and firm, about 10 minutes. Remove from the oven and reduce the heat to 160°C (325°F/Gas Mark 3).
5. Make the filling. Place the cream cheese, goat's cheese, lemon rind, lemon juice and vanilla

essence in a large mixing bowl. With an electric mixer, whisk until just smooth, scraping down the sides of the bowl.

6. Whisk in the sugar gradually and continue to whisk, then add the eggs, whisking until the mixture is very smooth. Pour the filling into the prepared crust.

7. Bake until the edges of the cheesecake are set and the centre is just slightly wobbly, about 60 minutes. Remove from the oven and place the tin on a wire rack to cool completely. When it is cool, cover and refrigerate in the tin for at least 6 hours or overnight.

8. Make the roasted pears. Preheat the oven to 200°C (400°F/Gas Mark 6).

9. Pare the pears, cut in half and scoop out the cores. Mix the butter, lemon juice, 15 ml (1 tablespoon) maple syrup and 60 ml (4 tablespoons) apple and pear juice in a medium baking dish. Bake for a moment or two until the butter melts, then mix.

10. Put the pears, cut-side down into the dish along with the rosemary sprigs. Bake for 15 minutes, then turn cut-side up and baste with the liquid. Continue to bake for another 5 minutes until the pears are just tender. Remove from the oven and allow to cool.

11. Put the remaining juice and remaining maple syrup into a small saucepan. Sieve the baking juices into the saucepan. Bring to the boil. Stir the cornflour mixture in and simmer, stirring, until the sauce thickens slightly, about a minute. Remove from the heat.

12. When you are ready to serve the cheesecake, remove it from the fridge and unmould onto a

serving plate. Cut into slices with a warm knife and serve with the sauce and a roasted pear half.

CHOCOLATE RASPBERRY ROULADE

You will need   **Serves 6**

    75 g (2$\frac{1}{2}$ oz) self-raising flour

    45 g (1$\frac{1}{2}$ oz) unsweetened cocoa powder

    4 large eggs, beaten

    115 g (4 oz) caster sugar, plus extra if necessary

    icing sugar to dust

    250 g (9 oz) fresh goat's cheese

    280 g (10 oz) fresh raspberries

1. Preheat the oven to 190°C (375°F/Gas Mark 5). Line a 30 x 23 cm (12 x 9-inch) swiss roll tin with parchment paper.
2. Sift the flour and cocoa powder into a bowl and set aside.
3. Put the eggs and sugar into a large bowl and whisk with an electric whisk for about 5 minutes, until very thick and pale; about the consistency of a mousse.
4. Sift the flour mixture into the egg, folding it in gently until it is thoroughly combined. Pour it into the prepared tin and level it with a knife.
5. Bake for 15 minutes, until firm. Remove from the oven.
6. Lay a sheet of parchment paper over a clean tea towel on a work surface and lightly dust with icing sugar.
7. Turn the sponge onto the sugared paper and peel off the liner. Roll the sponge up in the parchment and tea towel starting with one of the

short sides. Set aside until cool.

8. Whisk the goat's cheese in a bowl with a fork until smooth and add the raspberries, trying not to crush them too much. Taste and add the additional sugar if necessary. Unroll the cake, spread with the raspberry-cheese mixture and re-roll. Refrigerate until cold.

CINNAMON PEAR FROZEN YOGURT

You will need   **Makes about 1¹/₂ pints (900 ml)**

411 g (14 ¹/₂ oz) tinned pear halves in juice*

450 g (1 lb) fresh goat's yogurt

75 g (5 tablespoons) caster sugar

5 ml (1 teaspoon) vanilla essence

2.5 ml (¹/₂ teaspoon) ground cinnamon

1.25 ml (¹/₄ teaspoon) ground mixed spice

1. Drain pears, reserving 120 ml (4 fl oz) juice. Purée pears in a blender or food processor.

2. In a bowl, combine the pears, reserved juice, yogurt, sugar, vanilla essence, cinnamon and mixed spice. Mix well and pour into the container of an ice cream maker. Freeze according to the manufacturer's directions.

*This is also extremely successful made with 450 g (1 lb) fresh ripe pears, pared and cored, adding sugar as needed, water or fruit juice and a bit of lemon juice.

VANILLA ICE CREAM

You will need   **Makes about 600 ml (1 pint)**

4 eggs, separated

115 g (4 oz) icing sugar

2.5 ml (1/2 teaspoon) vanilla essence

360 ml (12 fl oz) fresh goat's milk

240 ml (8 fl oz) double cream

1. Whisk the egg yolks, vanilla essence and sugar in a bowl.
2. Meanwhile, bring the milk to the boil. Pour it over the egg yolk-sugar mixture, stirring constantly. Cool, then refrigerate until cold.
3. Whisk egg whites until stiff. Lightly whip the cream separately, then add both to the chilled milk mixture. Whisk well.
4. Pour the mixture into a shallow container and freeze until slushy.
5. Return the mixture to a bowl and whisk again.
6. Pour the mixture back into the container and re-freeze.
7. To serve, refrigerate for 30 minutes to soften slightly.

GLOSSARY

Abomasum — The fourth or true stomach of a ruminant where enzymatic digestion occurs
Afterbirth — The placenta and any foetal membranes expelled from a doe after kidding
Ash — The mineral matter of goat feed

Billy — A slang term for an uncastrated male goat
Billy rag — A cloth rubbed on a buck which is permeated with his odour and kept in a closed container. It is utilised by putting it under a doe's nose and observing her reaction to see if she is in heat
Bleating — Goat-speak
Bolus — A large oval medicinal tablet; also used to describe a chunk of cud
Buck — A male goat
Buckling — A young male goat
Browse — Bushy or woody plants; to eat such plants
Butting — The act of a horned goat bashing another goat or human

CAE — Caprine arthritis encephalitis — a serious type of virus that attacks goats, caused by a retrorivus.
Caprine — Pertaining to or derived from a goat
Chevon — Goat meat
Colostrum — The first thick, yellowish milk a goat produces after giving birth, rich in antibodies without which a newborn goat has little chance of survival
Concentrate — The non-forage part of a goat's diet, principally grain, but including oil, meal and other supplements high in energy and low in fibre

Conformation — The overall physical attributes of an animal; its shape and appearance
Cud — A ruminant's undigested food that the animal regurgitates to be chewed and swallowed again

Dam — Female parent
Dished face — The concave nose of the Saanen and Toggenburg breeds
Doe — A female goat
Doeling — A young female goat
Drenching — Giving liquid medication by mouth
Dry period — The time when a goat is not producing milk

Forage — The hay and/or grassy portion of a goat's diet

Gestation — The time between breeding and kidding (approximately 150 days)

Hay — Dried forage
Heat — The condition of a doe being ready to breed
Horn bud — Small bumps from which horns grow

In kid — Pregnant
In milk — Lactating

Ketones — Substances found in the blood of late-term pregnant goats suffering from pregnancy toxaemia
Ketosis — Over-accumulation of ketones in the body, responsible for pregnancy disease, acetomaemia,

twin lambing disease, or others that occur at the end of pregnancy or within a month of kidding
Kid — A goat under one year old; to give birth

Lactation — The period in which a goat is producing milk; the secretion or formation of milk
Legume — A family of plants having nodules on the roots bearing nitrogen-fixing bacteria, including alfalfa and clover

Mastitis — Inflammation of the udder, usually caused by an infection

Nanny — A slang term for a female goat — the preferred term is doe

Omasum — Part of a ruminant's stomach, sandwiched between the reticulum and the abomasums

Parturition — The act of giving birth
Predator — An animal that lives by killing and eating other animals
Polled — Hornless

Ration — Total feed given to an animal during a 24-hour period
Rennet — An enzyme used to curdle milk and make cheese
Reticulum — The second compartment of a ruminant's stomach
Rumen — The first large compartment of the goat's stomach where fibre is broken down

Ruminant — An animal with a multi-compartmental stomach

Rumination — The process whereby a cud or bolus of rumen contents is regurgitated, re-chewed and re-swallowed

Rut — The period during which a male goat has the desire to breed

Scour — Persistent diarrhoea in young animals

Scrapie — The goat and sheep version of mad cow disease

Service — Mating

Sire — Male parent; to father

Standing heat — The period when a doe will accept a buck for mating

Straw — Dried plant matter (usually oat, wheat or barley leaves and stems) used for bedding

Strip — To remove the last milk from the udder

Strip cup — A cup into which the first squirts of milk from each teat is directed, which will show any abnormalities which might be in the milk

Tattoo — Permanent identification of animals produced by placing indelible ink under the skin, generally in the ear

TDN — Total digestible nutrient; the energy value of the feed

Udder — An encased group of mammary glands provided with a teat

Udder wash — A dilute chemical solution, usually an iodine compound for washing udders before milking

Wether — A castrated buck
Whey — The liquid remaining when the curd is removed from curdled milk when making cheese
Worming — Using chemicals or herbs to rid an animal of internal parasites